Foreword

I have loved music for as long as I can remember. Quite frankly, all music. The sound of music. The feelings I get when listening. The memories it creates from moments shared. And the benefit of those moments becoming more significant when reminiscing about them years later. I would imagine, this same love was the driving force behind my chosen career path for over 20 years. I got my first on air radio job in 1998 with a small jazz radio station in Charlotte NC. I then went on to have my very own show at CBS Radio in the same market and have not looked back since. My experiences in the radio industry have put me in front of many faces and taken me to many places. I've been able to do everything from interviewing the biggest names in entertainment and hosting major events to working with local homeless shelters and creating programs to ensure that school teachers were acknowledged for their hard work and dedication. This same love and enthusiasm for music and community is the bridge that brought Jamie Brown into my life not so long ago. It was at a dinner gathering among mutual friends in Las Vegas that we met. We were introduced. Her warm and bubbly personality was immediately felt. Her charm and caring energy were pleasant. Her smile lit up the room. I knew at that point I had gained a new friend. As I look back on that night, I realize I sold myself short. I gained more than a friend. I gained a family member.

That is why I am excited about this book. I know the author. I have seen and understand many of the challenges she has faced. The losses she has experienced. And the disappointments she has had to accept. But most importantly, I have seen her unwavering faith and how she has overcome her challenges and continues to do so, even today. This book is a true reflection of Jamie and all that she is. It is a passion project full of truth, transparency, and honesty. In the Middle of It All will motivate, inspire, and empower you to walk into your own greatness and purpose. I encourage you to read every word, consider every thought, and enjoy getting to know this extraordinary person as she takes you on this life journey chronicling her early years until now seeing how God has watched over her to fulfill his purpose. I have no doubt that you will be energized and moved. Enjoy...

---- Preston Miles, Radio Personality / Entertainer

God has put on my heart I will be writing this book that I have chosen to call it "In the middle of it all" because it speaks to where I am and where God is gradually pulling me out of. I want it to be funny, witty and a must read so that people get drawn into my story without wanting to put it down. I want to be transparent about my life and add all the things that shaped me and made me who I am today. Here are a few scriptures that will be incorporated as I write this book and go through my life and write my testimony within this writing. My story is one of grace and redemption and the power of God at work in my life from the beginning to the end but I want to talk about what happens in the middle. People shy away from talking about the middle, it's not glamorous. In between you don't yet have all that God promised but you're not where you were in the past so what do you do? This is why I'm writing this book, I need to shed light on the middle of what you do when you're waiting. How do you cope when you have promises but not one thing is happening in your favor? I have these questions swirling around in my head and I talk to the Lord everyday about them. So I want to help all my people in the middle...

2 Corinthians 6:6

By purity, by knowledge, by long suffering, by kindness, by the Holy Spirit, by sincere love

1 Timothy 5:2

Older women as mothers, younger women as sisters, with all purity

Job 22:30

He will even deliver one who is not innocent; Yes he will be delivered by the purity of your hands.

Proverbs 22:11

He who loves purity of heart and has grace on his lips, The king will be his friend

1 Timothy 4:12

Let no one despise your youth, but be an example to believers in word, in conduct, in love, in spirit, in faith, in purity.

Proverbs 31:10-17

God showed me that I'm not a wife after I get married but He prepares me to be one while I'm waiting. I want to be a good steward over every gift God has given me and I want to be pure and clean before the Lord and an acceptable gift to His precious son when His timing is right. I want to document my journey in such a way that it is relatable to other women both young and old and that my humor and candor be able to give women the guidance they need through the word of God.

Proverbs 8:34

Blessed is the man who listens to me, Watching daily at my gates, Waiting at the posts of my doors.

Romans 8:23

Not only that, but we also who have the first fruits of the Spirit, even we ourselves groan within ourselves, eagerly waiting for the adoption, the redemption of the body.

Introduction

I want to talk about my journey, I don't want to talk about the happy ending but I want to talk from the perspective of what happens in the middle, your past is gone and your future hasn't yet happened what happens in the middle? That is what I want to talk about. I want to speak to the frustrations and disappointments in between. When you're in the waiting room it's hard to hear instructions from heaven. When you're in the holding tank you just have been put in this place of waiting, the information is sparse but the anxiety is high because not knowing is a nail biter.

This is when faith and trust needs to be on 10 because you want to blindly believe that everything God promises is coming but what is the timeline again Lord? I received all this prophetic word, a million confirmations and it's been almost 2 yrs? I know your word doesn't come back void Lord. I know people in the bible have waited a lot longer than that for things that are so much more dire. I just want my own stable place to live that is all I'm not asking because I have already done that, I am standing on His word that says I am a joint heir with Christ Jesus and I am no longer an orphan but I have been adopted into the family and I can cry Abba Father and come to his throne boldly to obtain mercy in the time of need. I am proclaiming every word that He said about me and my situation one of my favorite scriptures to stand on is:

Proverbs 3:5-6

Trust in the Lord with all your heart and lean not on your own understanding; In all your ways acknowledge Him and He will direct your path

Psalms 77:8,9

Has his mercy ceased forever? Has his promise failed forevermore? Has God forgotten to be gracious? Has He in anger shut up His tender mercies?

I feel like David when He is asking these types of questions, where you at Lord? Did I come too late, is this not going to come to pass?

Then He reminds me in all his glory and splendor the promise He gave Abraham.

Galatians 3:29

And if you are Christ's, then you are Abraham's seed and heirs according to the promise.

Our wonderful sovereign God loves to keep us hanging on the edge, He cuts it close! But as with Issac he always has a ram in the bush. I have seen so many miracles performed in my life even when I wasn't living right His mercies endure forever and His grace was definitely sufficient. So this brings me back to the Waiting room, Lord I know your word is true, your not a man that you should lie neither the son of man that you should repent so if you said it then it has to come to pass.

So Lord I know all these things but things just aren't moving, I have all these amazing promises, I have had dreams and visions and everything but I don't see anything yet. Got me out here looking crazy, I moved across the country only to be without a permanent place to live. Come on Lord this can't be part of the plan, is it? So I wait because I just have a word. I am definitely in great company though all the greats had to wait, Abraham, Job, Elijah Sarah, Elizabeth everyone waited for something so I didn't feel lonely we were all in the waiting room at one point.

So the waiting begins. I know what was spoken now, I wait, it's easy to get the promises and get all excited by what is about to happen, but when waiting is your only option, what do you do? Well let me give you a few more scriptures that may take the edge off the situation.

Hebrews 11:17-22

By Faith Abraham, when he was tested offered up Isaac, and he who had received the promises offered up his only begotten son, of whom it was said, "In Issac your seed shall be called", concluding that God was able to raise him up, even from the dead, from which he also received him in a figurative sense. By Faith Issac blessed Jacob and Esau concerning things to come. By Faith Jacob, when he was dying, blessed each of the sons of Joseph, and worshipped, leaning on the top of his staff. By Faith Joseph, when he was dying, made mention of the departure of the children of Israel and gave instructions concerning his bones.

This is the Faith and promise hall of fame. I mean these guys had some serious stuff happening in their lives and their faith never wavered no matter what was happening so it's definitely encouraging. Now fast forward 2019 I'm back in my waiting room trying to make sense of all my promises, I keep checking on my faith. It took some hits, it was just resuscitated after the last blow so I'm watching through the window as they do CPR and have the crash cart working on my faith.

It took a few hits, It's on life support and I have to wake up out of this spiritual coma the enemy is trying to put me in. I will stand on God's promises and make sure I come out of this with my faith intact. My confessions only are the word of God and I will not allow the enemy to have me look at my circumstances and tell me I won't make it. Ok my faith is off life support and is now in Stable condition I am allowing God to do all that he needs to in order to bring me back to a place of believing, and knowing. No matter what happens it can not steal my promise. Even now when it rains we still see a rainbow which was the promise God made to Noah so I know his promises will stay true for generations.

Philippians 4:12

I know how to be abased, and I know how to abound. Everywhere and in all things I have learned both to be full and to be hungry, both to amount and to suffer need.

It's so easy to get everything we need from the word of God in the darkest of times God has a scripture that aligns with every one of our circumstances and situations.

Hebrews 11:1-2

Now faith is the substance of things hoped for and the evidence of things not seen. For by it the elders obtained a good testimony.

This passage of scripture has been given to me countless times during this journey and I had to keep it hidden in my heart because situations and circumstances had me looking at things like...seriously is this really happening right now? How many times Lord will I have to move? When is my permanent home coming? I'm waiting, I'm standing on every word and promise and each circumstance just keeps showing me that it's not happening. But I walk by Faith and not by sight right Lord? That is what your word says, I have to believe it first then I will be able to see it. So I know that God your ways of doing things are not at all like ours. We truly live in a parallel universe where if we sow in tears we will reap in joy. I'm back in the waiting room. My Faith is in stable condition not completely out of the woods yet. This last episode was a big one, I lost my car and job all at once so now I feel like that just pushed me back 5 steps and I had made a few strides. Now the questions come again. Was I really supposed to come out here? Did you really call me here across the country to Las Vegas, NV the vacation capital of the world, does anyone really live here? I'm having this conversation with God in my head. I'm still trying to figure out what is going on. The lies that the devil is trying to tell me, that I don't belong here Lie #1 That I was better off in Delaware lie #2 and the biggest lie of them all, that he has the upper hand lie #3 so now I'm in an all out war. This is war and I'm clothed in my armor and I'm ready for battle who does this devil think he is messing with, I'm a child of the King, I'm a royal priesthood, My father owns the cattle on a thousand hills, he will supply all my needs according to His riches in glory through Christ Jesus. That's what the word says, I'm pumped now I'm ready to chop that devil's head right off, but I'm still in the waiting room. I have big faith, I'm steadfast and unmovable, I can quote every scripture and I have my warrior clothes on. But I'm still in the waiting room with my faith in stable condition as soon as it gets better, another attack and my faith takes a hit. I'm thankful for all the small victories and blessings that are coming my way.

1 Timothy 6:6

Now godliness with contentment is great gain

What a powerful scripture! I'm content, I'm full of joy, I'm obedient, I'm doing everything God is

telling me to do. But I'm back in the waiting room, watching my faith be hooked up to machines to keep it alive, I'm going to church, I'm even serving, feeding the hungry, serving the homeless, ministering and praying for everyone. I'm so happy for them as I see their prayers become answered and God just blessing them I'm so full of joy for them! But I'm back in the waiting room. I have all this word down in my heart, I have crazy faith, I have become long suffering, full of love and I'm preparing myself for everything God has for me but I'm still in the waiting room.

Chapter 1

The Flash back

I know God wants me to tell my truth and my story so that it can bless someone that may have had similar things happen and think God can't use you, well think again. Let's take a trip down my memory lane so I can go back to give you a little history so that all these things I'm saying make sense and we can tie it all up. So I was born in 1978 on one of the coldest and snowiest days in January the 22nd to be exact I came into this world on a Sunday which should have told me I was destined to be a chosen one, I made it! I was born in Reading PA which is about 45 minutes North of Philly and back in the day was known as the Outlet capital of the country. Now if you look up Reading we were top 10 Poorest cities in America. So I came from humble beginnings and clearly I'm just a kid from Reading that wasn't ever supposed to make it out but God had a different plan. It was touch and go because the two before me weren't as lucky, see let me explain my grandparents were old school Italians and having a black grandchild was an embarrassment to the family so my mom aborted 2 kids before me. They told her that they would disown her if she brought any black kids into the family. Many times while pregnant they would push her out the back door so no one would see her because they knew her boyfriend was black. So here I come into this cold world, on a cold day in January my mom had to walk to the ambulance because there was too much snow on our block. There was opposition from the very start, the devil started early trying to take me out my mom went to get another abortion with me but was too far along so I was coming whether my grandparents liked it or not. At one point my mother was going to adopt me out but couldn't go through with it. So I'm here in all my melanin glory!

Well they didn't like it apparently, according to my mom they wouldn't bring my brother or sister to see me in the hospital and wouldn't hold me or even touch me because I was too dark (so they said) so I came into the world being rejected, never felt good enough because of the color of my skin. My dad showed up 2 days after I was born. He was a little busy, at the time with his many women and who knows what else at that time in his life.

I'm sure this hurt my mother and I could feel this hurt and pain even as an infant because I always felt like she took out on me the disappointment she felt for him. So I grew and flourished in a very hostile environment. I have an older brother, and an older sister. I have 3 brothers from my dad but I am my mom's youngest child. At the time I was my dad's youngest child and only girl. Still to this day I'm my dad's only daughter. I grew up in the Glenside projects in Reading Pa. The projects were all I knew I was born with and then we moved to those homes while

I was still an infant. I didn't know being in the projects meant we were living in poverty, this was my family we all had the same things some more than others our house didn't look like a normal project house my mom loved to decorate and she was extremely clean so there was that. My dad was a hustler from my earliest memories of him. He had a real job but that didn't stop him from making part time business transactions at any of the April's bars on the Northside of town, 6th ward we affectionately call it.

I can remember things as far back as one yr old no one believes me but My impeccable ability to remember things I think was a Divine gift. I can remember sitting in a high chair in my grandmother's house with a birthday hat on and not because I saw the pic. I remember being there and eating some cake on my First birthday.

For the brevity of this chapter my father and mother didn't get along very well I don't recall any sweet affections between the two of them and then after the women, drugs and my mothers crazy outbursts of violence my dad had had enough so he left when I was 3 yrs old I can remember sitting them both down and sitting in between them and telling my dad he couldn't go and he was going to stay but it was all too much for him and he left anyway and this would be my first real heartbreak and feelings of abandonment and rejection. I didn't really understand why my dad left and for years I thought it was me. He was with my mom at this point for 10 yrs so I felt like he could have stayed a little longer for me. I didn't realize the level of dysfunction this relationship was on and all his staying would have done was make my life more miserable and hard. In my 3 yr old mind I thought why would he leave me? Doesn't he love me? I asked him to stay but he didn't so I'm not worth enough for him to stay. This was the beginning of my feelings of inferiority and I would continue on my adult life finding men that would do exactly what my father did, leave and reject me.

I started school When I was 5 and I was in Kindergarten at this point my dad was gone and moved on and my mom was angry and bitter I didn't know what that was back then she was just mean, and very verbally and physically abusive to both myself and my older sister. She often would use the N word and tell me that she wished she would have aborted me too when she would get really mad at me because I guess I reminded her of my dad and that was a sore spot for her so she would go through periods where she didn't have a man and her daughters would pay the price. I want to stop here and talk about how powerful words are that are spoken, even though the person saying them may never really remember what they said. The person it's said to will carry that with them forever and it will affect and shape their lives. Very much like those words my mother spoke over my life shaped how I saw myself for decades after. My sister was like my second mom she was 8 yrs older than me and she really took care of me and made sure I was always ok, she would protect me when my mom and dad would fight she would always put her Walk man on my ears so I couldn't hear my mom yelling and cursing at my dad when he would want to pick me up. Now let me pause and explain to any millennials reading this what a Walkman is. It was our 80s version of having an IPod or MP3. It played the radio or a cassette tape and we had black foam headphones that came with it. I believe this is how music became very therapeutic for me over the years and everytime I needed to escape it would be to a book or music. So one day my mom finally let my dad pick me up and I ended up with one of his girlfriends and she took me to school shopping, now what's wrong with this you say? Nothing in theory but this wasn't just any shopping spree. As we were heading to our destination we were driving in the car and all of a sudden she pushed my head down into the seat and told me to stay hidden because she didn't want her parents to see me, She told me her parents didn't like black people and she didn't want them to see her with me. Here we go again. This was sounding all too familiar. I didn't understand what was happening. I'm 5 yrs old and don't understand why my skin color is such an issue. She was a Caucasian woman as well my dad had a fetish at that time for caucasian females. This was still risky business in the early 80s and being a mixed kid was difficult; you just never seem to fit in anywhere. I started to resent my dad for choosing these situations and not thinking about my feelings or well being. After we passed her parents we headed to the mall. She buys me new shoes, new clothes and a lunch box. It was Strawberry Shortcake, my favorite character at the time. We are all done shopping and she takes a drive to see if she can find my dad and we end up at a bar now it's like 1983 and this bar is called the Touchdown all the neighborhood people would frequent this place. It just so happen that we didn't find my dad but we did find his other girlfriend and she came to the car and wanted to fight with my dads other girlfriend that took me shopping and a baseball bat was pulled out and as the ladies fought over the bat I'm in the front seat watching this all go down and get hit in the chin. Oh boy now I'm bleeding and this lady has to take me home to my crazy mother and explain what took place. In today's society CPS would have been on the scene and everyone would have been in a lot of trouble but what was even scarier than that was my mother. I can see the fear on this lady's face and even though she was white she turned bright red and then a ghost white as we approached my house. She slowly walked me to the door concocting her story but she was at a disadvantage because someone at the bar that witnessed this had already called my mom and she was waiting at the door. She screamed at this lady and all I remember seeing was a phone flying at this woman's head and her running down our walkway holding her head in her hands and my mother screaming obscenities until I could no longer see the woman.

My dad was really in trouble now; she already didn't want me with him because she was the president of the petty, scorned babymomma club, she was actually the founder of this great organization, but now my dad and his entourage gave my mom every reason to be super petty. The original Petty Patty was in full effect and I remember how she would have one of her friends take her to the bar, after she called there a thousand times and my dad stopped answering and would just drop me off and leave me at the bar! My dad would teach me to play pool, and I would drink soda, it's the 80s no one cares that I'm at the bar. Today both my parents would have been locked up CPS would have definitely been involved. I was literally a pawn in the game of revenge between my parents. The next weekend I find myself at my dad's other girlfriends house and once again he isn't there and I'm left alone with her and her family but I loved her daughters and they have become my sisters and treated me with the utmost respect. She ended up braiding my hair for my picture day at school and that was actually a fun weekend.

I'm coming home all proud and happy hoping my mom would be happy that no one was attacked and my hair looked cute, she didn't even have to do it for about 2 weeks. She did find a reason to say something, I was too happy and she didn't like that so she found a reason to complain. She was mad at me. I didn't know what I did when I was 5, at this point I know that something is wrong with my mother but I didn't know what at the time, I will later find out my mother suffered from mental illness. In today's society she suffers from an extreme anxiety disorder and possibly narcissistic behaviors, there may be a touch of Bipolar disorder as well. She also was very broken and hurt from her life and childhood, my grandmother was not the nicest either, she would always say she wished she would have never had my mother because she almost died giving birth, and to hear that as a child was not healthy and she just repeated that behavior with me. My mother told me she had a nervous breakdown at 11 yrs old. This my friends is what us good church going folks call a generational curse. I have broken this with my daughter and my sons in Jesus name. They know they are loved and accepted and it doesn't matter where they go or what they do, they are mine and I love them unconditionally.

Needless to say I had a hard time trying to understand why my father left me with this crazy woman, she couldn't find anything good in anything anyone did no matter what it was and she was scary. The way she treated my sister made me sad and scared for her and I ended up on the receiving end of one of her outbursts when she threw a tupperware sewing box at my sister and it hit me right in the face. This is why I would hide when my sister would get a beating because I know she couldn't have done anything bad enough to deserve the whooping she was getting, it made me sad for her and scared that if she saw me she would hit me too just for watching. I never saw anyone treat their daughter like that, it was like my mother was hitting her and taking all the frustration and anger she felt toward herself or her life out on my sister. I know this hurt and disappointed my sister because all she ever wanted was to hear my mom say something nice to her, to show her that she really loved her. Not to mistreat her or act out in jealousy or anger but really love her and care for her as a mother should have. Now don't be mistaken, even though I was young I was beaten as well. My mother beat me with an umbrella at just 3 yrs old. She would always say that I was hard headed and that a hard head made a soft butt that is why she was beating me. This was the logic of abuse back then, that today would have kids taken away and parents locked up. Let me pause here and say child abuse of any kind is not acceptable and this is something I will fight with all of my God given skills to eradicate. The system that houses the children that are removed from these situations isn't much better it's an extremely flawed system. It needs to change and I'm thankful that God is giving me the wisdom and strength to do something different. Fast forward a few years and things for my mother went from bad to worse.

So at this point I'm about 7 and my mom decides to start writing this guy in jail and at first we were like ok she has a pen pal cute but when we went to a Mosque and I had to go in the back door and take off my shoes I was feeling some type of way. What was happening mother? We are not Muslims nor do I with my

Catholic school self want to convert to the Islamic faith. So I'm refusing to take off my shoes and there is quite a commotion at the door, I'm getting death stares but I'm holding my ground, what if someone steals my shoes? I was not having any of it, so needless to say we never made it in because I was being disrespectful is what the man at the door said. I was ok with that because I didn't want to go there anyway. Of course I got yelled at for embarrassing her and she probably would have hit me too if we were not in front of folks. This man must be special. I was thinking of going to all this trouble for a religion that you know nothing about. That this man will abandon the moment his feet hit some freedom. I saw it all before living in the hood gives you this insight these guys have their jailhouse religion to pass the time or for protection and then come out and forget all about it. We start to go to the prison to visit this man and once again I'm protesting the whole way I don't like it. We have to travel too far and I had to leave my sister and I wanted to be at home not taking a train and a bus to visit a man in prison I didn't know.

Chapter 2

The visit

We finally reach the prison and it's our turn to visit and my mom is super happy to see this man, I had the stank face didn't know him, didn't like him and he would not be my stepfather, my dad may not have been around but at least I knew him and he was still my dad didn't need a replacement. As I sit there I'm not understanding why my mom is wearing a white dress and they have all these extra people on this visit. My mom is marrying this bum, I can't believe it she is really marrying this jailbird at this point I'm just sitting in my full blown attitude. Little did I know at the time this union would change my life forever. My dislike of him was actually discernment and it would all unfold when he was released.

I couldn't believe who my mother was turning into she had became a full fledge agoraphobe she never left the house anymore she would just write this man nonstop and wait for his call to run our phone bill up, and I couldn't understand why she loved this guy so much she barely knew him. He would be released in the summer of 1987 and this would be quite the homecoming. This man wasn't out a month before he started to use crack cocaine. We are in the very thick of the crack era, Reagan is president and Nancy is telling us all just to say no, I truly believe this guy missed that memo because he was hooked. I remember coming home from school early one day. It was a rainy day I want to say in September because summer had ended and I was back at school. At this point I'm in the 4th grade and I'm almost 9 I took a nap and woke up and my mom and I started to organize her plant books, I loved flowers and I enjoyed learning about them. We haven't seen the husband in a few days so it was actually nice not having him around. But then there was a knock at the door, he was back but something in his eyes looked dark and scary. I couldn't put my finger on it then but now I know that crack demon had a hold of him and he was possessed. Him and my mother started to argue and he admitted to cheating on my mom with a woman of the night and they had been out for days getting high. My mom became furious as she was obviously getting flashbacks about my dad and his womanizing nature and just flipped out on this man and grabbed an 8 in kitchen knife and started stabbing this man's coat. I started to yell, but no one was listening. I was so scared and instantly felt helpless. I was there alone, my sister had moved out and with her boyfriend they had my nephew and he was a baby so my sister wasn't there to protect me anymore so I had to think quickly on my feet. How can I stop this fight? I'm only 9yrs old and I never saw my mom get this mad. I was so scared I could feel my stomach tighten like I was about to throw up. I saw this man's eyes become wide and crazy and he starts to hit my mother back and she drops the knife. At this point he is boxing my mom like she was an unsuspecting adversary. She had no more defense. He was relentlessly punching my mom in the face and she was literally walking with each blow and he beat her from our living room until he basically knocked her out in our backyard. I just stood there watching this all happen, not able to speak. I couldn't even process what I just saw. When I went outside to see if my mother was still alive, I saw him run away like a coward and left me there to pick my mother's lifeless body off the lawn. I still to this day couldn't understand how I got the strength to get my mother's body off the lawn and into the house I know angels were helping me now because she was beaten severely and going in and out of consciousness. I called my sister and her and my brother came down to get me, my mom was taken away in an ambulance and my brother took me to their house so I could try and sleep. Sleep wasn't my friend that night or any other night for the next few weeks. I had nightmares, and all of a sudden I had this sad feeling that never went away. Nothing that used to make me happy or get me excited had an effect. I was just sad and scared all the time and I didn't know how to articulate that. I was 9 yrs old, just a little girl that didn't know how to process my mother being beaten almost to death and me thinking she was dead. Then walking around with her after the fact brought on an embarrassment and shame that I didn't even understand. She had bruises and lumps all over her face. It was horrifying to look at, and because she kept telling people lies instead of the truth of what really happened. I just kept trying to understand why she would try to protect a man that almost killed her. I was screaming on the inside. I wanted to just blurt out her jailbird drug addict husband did this right in front of me! I just couldn't believe she wasn't telling the truth and why was he not back in jail I didn't understand why my mother allowed this to happen to her. This sadness and depression In mental health terms in 2020 would have been as follows I would have been diagnosed with Post Traumatic Stress Disorder or PTSD for short. The depression was a byproduct of everything I had witnessed but wouldn't even recognize that until adulthood.

I thought surely this would be the end of Mr jailbird woman beater so I could be confident that my mom couldn't be this desperate. Surely her decision making would change since this happened , she would never want this to happen again, she would not want to put her terrified 9 yr old daughter through anything else. Well my mother takes him back! Let me pause here and talk to any woman that was abused or that is currently in an abusive relationship of any kind GET OUT NOW! You can do it. God will help you and open doors for you just take the first step. Please call the National Domestic Violence Hotline 1-800-799-7233 and ask for help before it's too late. Do not let your current circumstances or any lie the enemy has ever spoken in your ear to have you believe that you aren't worthy, God loves you and if you are saved you are His daughter and He wants nothing but the best for you! I couldn't believe this woman, this had to be a nightmare I'm going to wake up from right? She really isn't going to live with this man again? He apologized she said, he is just heartbroken by what he did, he said he would never hit me again, classic abuser excuses. I just stood looking at both of them like they had grown 3 extra heads and those heads were talking in a different language only they could understand. I ran to my room and started pumping music through my headphones. I didn't want to hear anything else, I didn't want to see anything else. I just wanted to be far away from all of this. One thing I knew for sure if that man ever laid one paw on me my dad, uncles and cousins would be there so quick that man wouldn't be able to get out fast enough. Like most women beaters they don't want any real static with a man they are cowards and they want to pick on a seemingly weaker person. I'm sure somewhere in his life he was bullied or mistreated. I think he knew that so he tread lightly with me, my family was big and my dad wasn't a violent man but he definitely had a goon squad ready to pounce on a child abuser. Weeks go by and it seems calm but I never trusted him and I just knew this was the calm before the storm. Because all the anger and rage in that man's body he wasn't going to stop until he killed my mother. So on a beautiful spring day I was getting ready for school as I always did, but today felt different. I had a very uneasy feeling. Something wasn't quite right so I went into my moms room to let her know I was leaving and there sat Mr. Jailbird woman beater with a small revolver in his hand, it was a black snub nose with a pearl handle. He was forbidding anyone to leave this bedroom he was paranoid, and coming down from a high and he was extremely dangerous. I just started telling jokes and making light of this situation, so angry with my mom for putting us back in this situation now he was planning on killing all of us. Great I didn't do anything but be this crazy lady's daughter and I'm clearly getting the short end of the stick. I started to talk to God and asked Him to protect us and get us out of this safely. I'm joking and telling funny stories and just trying to lighten this mood. All of a sudden he lets me call my grandpa and allows him to come pick us up. Needless to say my mom went to get a PFA against him Protection From Abuse order after this incident. So I thought we were safe because now she wasn't going to allow him back in, my grandpa came with his shotgun in a bag ready to blow this man away. Now my mother's terrible decision making has affected me, my grandfather and the rest of the family. Once the PFA was in place he was not allowed within 30 feet of us or the cops would come and lock him up. Good I thought that is where he belongs anyway they should have never let him out. Now my fear and anxiety was on a 10 every noise I heard made me jump, and I couldn't eat. My stomach was always upset. I had to start taking medicine to calm my stomach so I could sleep. One night while all was seemingly quiet we heard glass breaking and low and behold there was a brick right through our window this man was terrorizing us, I was always scared and why didn't my mother see that. She didn't see how her choices were affecting me. My mother picked a real winner I tell you my fear was amplified once again, then we find out he stabbed his new girlfriend with a screwdriver and now was back in jail for the first time in the last year I was petrified to even fall asleep, and God heard my pleas My prayers were answered, Our nightmare was finally over.

Chapter 3

The Recovery

I don't know if I had ever really recovered from that ordeal but I managed to move on with my life and grow up. I was very popular and had a lot of friends. I became a class clown, or a comedian if you will. It was a skill I learned from my time in the diffusion tank, attempting to lighten an otherwise somber occasion with comic relief. I became good at roasting my friends and busting on them as we used to call it. I don't think my mom ever really recovered from her ordeal; she had a lot of damage physically and emotionally. I'm going to take the time out to say that although I didn't realize then, my mother was extremely broken, because she came from a mother that was verbally abusive and she just never was validated in her childhood and looked for that validation elsewhere, so when you don't see your worth as a person, because of how you see yourself and dealing with your form of verbal abuse from your own mother you don't know how to treat anyone else. This was the real issue and it was never brought up or even realized and became a generational curse that I later would break. Her lack of dealing with her own pain and brokenness started boiling over onto me in the form of nastiness and clinginess if that was even possible she wouldn't let me go anywhere but didn't want me around and if I was out with my friends she would come looking for me and embarrass me. She was very miserable and mean to me she had a string of boyfriends here and there that were just dead beat drug addicts that didn't last long. She had this uncanny knack for finding the most broken man and trying to fix them up and all she did was make them worse. Let's be clear, two broken people never fix anything. All that does is make a bad situation terrible. What I have learned and seen in my mother's life was that she was unconsciously attracting what she thought she deserved.

By this time I was in middle school and having the time of my life, I still struggled with depression and extreme sadness although I would think about what it would be like to go to heaven I never would of contemplated suicide, I was too afraid of death and I didn't want to sin against God. I was told that it was a sin to kill yourself growing up in the Catholic church. Then I started going to a Christian church when I was about 12 and accepted Jesus as my personal savior but the sadness and depression only got worse, I just wanted the pain to stop. I wanted to be anywhere else but where I was and I prayed that God would help me deal with my anguish. I just plastered a smile on my face and joked my way out of my pain and anguish. I became very good at masking my hurt and just pushing down everything that bothered me, but as I got older I became very angry, I was a ticking time bomb and didn't even know it. Things weren't the best at home I fought with my mom constantly, I just wanted the freedom to be a kid and have fun with my friends but she just couldn't allow that, her misery wants company.

So at around 15 I started to rebel. I knew that I had to get away from her one way or another. I had enough of the abuse and the control I just wanted to enjoy my life and do normal teenager things. My sister who at this time was married, and had already moved into her 5 bedroom home offered to take me in to help my mom. I was the happiest I had been in a long time, and my sister let me go out with my friends and have fun so I was out all the time, started going to clubs underage and dancing and hanging with some unsavory friends. I was still a virgin at this point and had no desire to have sex with anyone but plenty of guys wanted to have sex with me. I had one particular incident where one of the guys I was dating, who may I add was too old to be dating a 16 yr old decided he wanted to show me what oral sex was about. This man then pulled his pants down and chased me around the house with his penis out! I was horrified and I kept screaming as I locked myself in the bathroom, I was going to call my brother. I made sure to let him know if he didn't pull his pants up and leave I was calling my brother. He eventually left and never got any of my virgin goodies, but it was scary because I never had anyone become that aggressive with me. My mom got word that I was doing pretty good with my sister, I was working after school and I was happy, well she couldn't have that and started doing very vindictive things To my sister and she couldn't handle the stress and sent me back home. I will never forget it. It was Easter Sunday 1993 I was devastated. I did not want to go back to my moms just the thought of it made me instantly sad and angry. I cried all the way home and my sister cried too. She didn't want me to leave but had no choice, my mom was still the boss at this point I had no interest in being there so I started being extremely rebellious being mouthy and just didn't care and stopped going to school and lost my job. I had given up and was sent to an alternative school and I was so smart, the work we were doing in that alternative school I did in 5th grade. I was reading at 3 yrs old, went to Catholic school and was way ahead of all my classmates. My dream was to be a pediatrician when I was little so I had the intellectual ability but my circumstances were choking those dreams out of me. So I recall getting into a huge fight with my mom and ran away. I was 16 yrs old and I was now on the street, couldn't go back to my sisters and my grandparents wouldn't take me in because my mom had bad mouthed me so I had nowhere to go. I was literally staying in hallways and trying to stay at friends houses. Ended up in some precarious situations that caused me to trade sex for a place to stay and before I knew it in April of 1994 I would lose my virginity to someone that was 20 yrs old because I needed to stay with him I had no one else. I felt sick to my stomach. I vowed to remain a virgin until marriage, and here I was basically giving away my treasure for a warm bed. I felt like Esau giving away his birthright for a bowl of soup. I felt so worthless and the very thing I identified myself with, became the very thing that sunk me right back into depression once it was gone. This would be a pattern over the next few years once I started to sleep around. That is just what I did. I gave my precious body away just in hopes that they may decide to love me, or give me any type of attention. I craved so much, but it was the opposite the more I gave the emptier I felt and I couldn't shake this feeling of guilt and shame that was an all too familiar feeling. Just not feeling worthy so I would just sleep with anyone that smiled and showed me interest. I'm about to put myself out there but I had slept with close to 70 people by the time I was 21 my brokenness was in full swing. The enemy had me right where he wanted me and my identity was in the toilet and I had no value in myself or my body. I was just looking for that love and acceptance and wanted someone to just show me that they cared. While I was on the street I gained an unlikely ally, my very first crush had taken an interest in me. I can't lie this was a daydream come true because I always had a huge crush on him. He was gorgeous and I was in love with him since I was 11. He would come looking for me while I was on the block, it would sometimes be close to midnight and I would see that gray Jetta pull up and I felt like Julia Roberts in pretty woman this was my knight in shining armor and it was very romantic when I think about it. So he would take me home with him, once we got to his house he would take a bubble bath with me and we would talk and laugh and he would hold me and say sweet things to me. I really feel like God had used that situation to keep me protected on the streets. He was my angel at the time and I always felt loved and cared for when I was with him. I was really in love with him and I didn't care who knew I wanted to scream it from the rooftops how I felt with him but I knew I couldn't. No one could know our families would never understand. I was underage and he was with someone but the gravitational pull between us was unlike anything I ever felt for the first time I was being made love too this was not sex as usual.

It wasnt just about sex, we had history, he knew me and wanted me anyway I needed this, I craved it. I knew I wouldn't be able to be his real girlfriend but what he was giving me was all I needed for the moment. We had to be careful no one would find out he was 22 at the time and I was 16 and he had a girlfriend and his mom would be at work over night so I would fall asleep in his arms every night he would pick me up. It was magical to me at this stage of my life. It wasn't the most ideal situation but it kept me safe and I was really in love with him in a way I have never felt, it was definitely a forbidden love which made me more drawn to it. To support myself while out on the street I sold weed and heroin our bags were called Overdose the bags had a skull and crossbones on the front I will never forget that ,seeing these people coming up to us that were dopesick, with sores and scabs all over them it was hard to look at and I knew I couldn't do that for long. Didn't mind selling the weed that was usually just to my homies and people they knew so It was easy. Then I started staying with an old friend I grew up with who was more like a sister and she got me connected with a club she worked at that would hire me to dance even though i was underage. I had the perfect body for stripping and not much shame in my game, I was wild and crazy and didn't care much about myself so this wasn't hard. I still had daydreams, thoughts of me and my crush because I was a hopeful romantic. I always dreamed he would just show up and take me out of my misery and just love me the way they did in my romance novels I used to read. He was a bright spot in what was going on in my life and would be a very significant part of my story. I found out in January of 1995 that I was pregnant and had no idea at the time who the father was so this was so scary and I was in denial for months and would barely eat or anything. I slept a great deal trying to wrap my head around what was happening. God used this precious baby boy to save my life because I was a wild one out in those streets, remember the ticking time bomb of anger? Well I had exploded and was constantly fighting, now I wouldn't start these fights but I didn't back down and after a while I had a reputation I would fight anyone, male or female I Carried a razor blade in my mouth and wasn't afraid to use it. I was officially a gangsta and hung with nothing but drug dealers and street dudes they became my family. They looked out for me. I had dudes that would fight for me like I was their real sister and it felt good to have that type of support. My real family wasn't this attentive or protective so I felt more love on the street then at home. I helped hold the drugs and because I was underage the cops wouldn't search me so I would walk around with bundles of dope in my bra like nothing, would be up in these apartment buildings til 6 or 7 am hustling with my brothers. My mom was always out trying to find me and one night as I was visiting my friend she happened to be at the bar next to her house talking to a friend, as soon as she saw me she started yelling and grabbed me. I came out of my coat she had me gripped by, and jumped on my friends bike and got out of there! Once I found out I was pregnant I went back home after being in the street for about 6 months doing what I had to for survival. I thank God during this time he protected me from my simple mistakes and kept me from disease and death. I had lost a few friends while out there one was shot and the other was stabbed in the chest. One night after one of my many fights we actually went looking for these chicks because they disrespected me by coming to my block even though I beat her up we still had to retaliate. So as we drove to find these girls my boy ran a stop sign and got pulled over, no one in the car had a license and we got the car from one of the addicts that would exchange his car for drugs, we all were arrested that night for curfew and underage drinking. My homegirl that was of age took the rap for the open container and we were taken in for curfew so needless to say I didn't go back home by my own admonition. I was handcuffed to the chair at the station and they called my mother and here she came. Yelling and screaming at me and at this point she had a new boyfriend. This one I didn't mind. He wasn't bad and had a real job and was from Philly. He was quiet and way too nice for my mom. She would find a way to ruin this man's life with all her insecurity and brokenness. Faked a pregnancy and a miscarriage on this poor man put some methylate on her legs, now for those of you that do not know what that is it's an old school pain reliever for cuts and scrapes and turned red on your skin. She told that poor man this lie and had him believing it. I was disgusted. I got back home and things weren't any better but I decided to go back to school and get a job. It made a difference. I was staying busy and was not allowing my mother and her actions to get me down. I look back and see the hand of God at work in my life. I was literally looking for love and acceptance in all the wrong places, My obsession with romance novels didn't help, I was always expecting someone to come and rescue me and little did I know at the time someone already did and His name was Jesus. He went to the cross for my sins and rescued me from the wages of sin and death and if I only knew at the time how much He loved me and wanted to show me who I really was, that this imposter was in the place of the real person He created it would have changed my life forever.

Chapter 4

The arrival

My beautifully handsome firstborn son would come into this world at 5:30am on October 3 1995 after being 15 days late he was extremely comfy in that womb. This precious child would change my life forever, now I would be lying if I said that this was the happiest moment of my life, I was scared and I didnt know what I was doing I was only 17 and I was so afraid that I was going to be just like my mother was and it terrified me. I at least felt like this child would love me unconditionally because he is mine and I am his mother. There were times I felt he was better off without me and there were alot of times I chose to work or be away instead of doing all I could to be a good mother. The saddest thing for me is that I had brought this child into the world and would be a single mother. I told myself I never wanted my child to go through what I did not have a father and I vowed not to be part of the Bitter babymomma club, so it didn't matter if they left, I sure wouldn't be chasing them! I didn't know how I would be able to do this but what I did know was that I was going to love this baby like no one ever loved me, I was going to give him all the opportunities that i didn't have or wasn't given it took me a while and I went through a great deal during this process and the most trying was when I went to my best friends graduation. We both came from the same place and not the most desireable circumstances but she made a choice and so did I. I was standing at her graduation in my prom dress i never Got to wear holding a baby on my hip while I watched her graduate, although I was extremely proud and happy for her, I was sad for myself because that was my graduating class too, I should have been walking across that stage with my classmates being young and free and starting the beginning of the rest of our lives instead i was raising another life and I felt as though now everything I wanted to accomplish would be that much harder to achieve.

I was trying to make sense of all of it, I would question God all the time, why did you give me this lady as a mother, why did my dad leave me at 3 why did all this happen the way it did God? I would not get those answers until I started seeking him. I was so broken and hurt and I needed some type of relief soon. My son was now about a year old and my mom started going back to church so I started to go with her, and the first time I really wanted to seek the Lord, anything had to be better than how I was living. I didnt think my problems would just clear up at once but I knew there was something to the Jesus thing and I wanted to give it a try and I was already 18 so I didn't need my mothers permission to go on my own. She was good for church hopping once things didn't go the way she expected them to go, she loved talking about me and trying to make me seem like the most terrible person, she never once took into consideration I was dealing with my own brokenness and anguish and just wanted relief. No one knew my heart the way God did and no one knew what I needed at that moment but God did, he sent me my spiritual parents that would start to pour into my life, love me and show me who I was in Christ. Now my story doesn't end there, it's only the beginning. I was getting a lot of word that I was trying to process, I didn't fully understand what was going on around me I was still an infant in the family of Christ so I started to make decisions like a child would, started sleeping with that Pastors son and he was good and married and it just became a huge scandal. The enemy was using all these attacks as a way to keep me from my true destiny. He attacked my identity and made me feel guilty and shameful as if God couldn't forgive me and this was just always going to be who I was no matter how much I wanted different. I didn't know at the time but 1 John 1:9 says' If we confess our sins, he is faithful and just to forgive us our sins and cleanse us from all unrighteousness. Men and relationships would prove to be Achilles heal throughout my life and the enemy would always use these familiar spirits just in different bodies. When I was 19 I met this man at the Getty Mart now for those that don't know that was like a 7-11 and this one happened to be on Greenwich Street in Reading now it is 1997 and I'm fresh off of having my baby, dealing with Daddy issues and in walks this 41 yrs old man that happens to be the Pastor of the church I was attending this is his brother. Now here I would insert the eye roll emoji if this was a text and hand over my face because I was a mess, a good ole mess and I am keeping it in the family. I was so embarrassed but didn't even know any better. Honestly this brokenness and need for love and attention and my self worth issues was driving me all of the way so I started seeing this man. Who had a live-in girlfriend and a baby who happened to be the same age as my son and they would even play together because he had him in the store and I would take my son with me as well. So we can already tell this situation is just another train wreck waiting to happen. It's like it all happened in slow motion. I saw the train coming but just couldn't get the car off the tracks fast enough and Bam there was. So this was a tumultuous situation. We move in together and the ex girlfriend comes to the house because now he is caught, we are both naked I have a sheet wrapped around myself and the babies are both sleeping. This chick had the nerve to say something about my son and all I remember is I was swinging on both her and her friend and at this point I'm naked and fighting and don't even care what you won't do is say one single thing about my son! Now I started boxing so my hits are real strategic and I'm trying to take these chicks heads off. I was still young, angry and always ready for a fight. I had so much growing to do but at this point this was my life 19 sleeping with a 41 yr old and trying to get my life. God was using every circumstance and situation in my life to show me how much He truly loved me and wanted to save me from myself. I would like to say that this was just a cake walk. After giving my life to the Lord it became harder and harder to navigate my life, the enemy was hitting me harder and harder at every turn. I had to get out of my mother's house again because she was just being completely ridiculous, especially after I started going to church without her and she could no longer manipulate the church folks about how terrible I was and all I was putting her through they knew it was her and not me. I started taking my GED classes and really started focusing on getting my life back on track because I knew education was key to finding the type of job that I needed to take care of my family. I found out in Aug of 1999 that I was pregnant with my second child so I definitely could not be living with my mother under any circumstances so I started to really push. Found a little place for me and my son, and passed my GED test and was able to get my drivers license. Things were finally coming together. I refused to bring another child in the world without what I needed and God came through. I was walking my son to school everyday and it was so cold I just kept telling him we will have our car soon baby dont worry, "He would cry because he was so cold but I just trusted that God would bless us He saw my press. I was waking up at 4:30 in the morning every day and walking to prayer. I needed God so bad and my desperation showed and He rewarded me. By the time my second son came I had my apartment, my car and my GED for the first time in a while I felt good about myself and what me and Jesus were accomplishing. Quickly because of all this good the enemy was coming, my ex boyfriend that I thought was my second son's dad showed up professing his love. He gave me all the feels because he made me feel like no matter what was going on he had my back and was going to help me raise my kids. Well this was great. I have been wanting a real family for such a long time and this would give my kids a chance not to grow up in the same dysfunction that I did so this made me happy, surely this was from the Lord. Wrong! This situation was straight from the pit of hell, I think the envelope was still smoking on the package it came in! Not even a few weeks went by and I figured out that he had nowhere to live and didn't really want to help he wanted to live off me and then once the paternity test proved he wasn't the father I didn't hear from him again for a while, but by this point all the blessings that I started to see were slipping away. I started looking at man again and started slipping back into my old promiscuous ways and stopped trusting God to provide. That is when God showed me the Lord gives and takes away and now my car has broken down and I couldn't afford to fix it. The electricity at my house was in my moms name and as soon as she got upset with me she turned it off, and I already was on the way to eviction because of my trust in the wrong thing and not taking care of my business too busy chasing this man. So one of my friends that I have met had an apartment it wasnt in the greatest part of town but it was a roof for me and my children because at this point I already had lost everything else so I was starting over again and this guy wasn't really charging me anything because the house needed some work.

Chapter 5

The shooting

This house kind of creeped me out from the beginning, something just didn't sit well with me but back then I didn't listen to my Holy Spirit guidance and I went along with what I thought was right and not realizing this devil was on my heels he knew the call God had on my life so he needed to stop it at all costs. I was just so oblivious to all of his schemes and tactics so I trusted all the wrong people. I was met with a proposition upon moving into that apartment, the neighborhood dealer had asked if he paid me if he can stash drugs in my basement now at this point my rent was like 300 a month and that's what he wanted to give me so I was set, so I thought this would turn out to be a fatal mistake. One night after coming home from school, the cops showed up at my door and said I called the police, I was like no officer I just got home and no one was here how could that be? I picked up my phone and it had no dial tone, this happened several times over the next few weeks of me being in this apartment. I didn't know then but this would be a very eerie calling card because I would eventually have to really dial 911 and it wouldn't be a false alarm this time.

 One of my friends thought it would be fun to stick up the dudes outside hustling, because at the time he actually was getting high and I didnt know he was my dude. We hung out and he looked out like a brother. He proceeded to stick this dude up at knife point and made him strip down to his boxers and took all his money and drugs and had this kid walking home half naked in the winter it was embarrassing. He really got punked and although we all laughed, I was smiling on the outside but deep down I was afraid this was going to come back in an ugly way on me, Now this devil is on my heels so he is trying to take me out completely he knows the moment I walked in those church doors that I had the potential to find out who I was in Christ and he couldn't have that or I was going to make his daily existence miserable. So later that day my mom came to pick up my oldest son, and my boyfriend took our dog to a friends house because the landlord was coming the next day and needed to get in. I didn't think that he would stay over there too and abandon me, so it was just myself and my son who at the time was about 7 months. He was sleeping and I was watching a TV show on forensics that was interesting but a bit creepy, there was an eerie silence in the air, I tried to shrug it off but I started to get a little scared. I got up to walk into the kitchen and the baby woke up and started crawling toward me and I picked him up and was about to dial my friends number when all of a sudden, shots rang out I dropped to the floor and covered the baby with my body and waited for those bullets to stop. It must have been about 10 to 15 of them before they finally stopped and now I had to access the damage and call the police. When I went out to the living room there was glass everywhere and holes in the window the size of oranges, but when i looked up not one bullet was anywhere on the floor it looked like someone pushed those bullets into the drop ceiling. I know now that it was my angels protecting me because the enemies plan was to kill me that night. The word says those weapons will form but they won't prosper. I saw that first hand. I went to church that Sunday and I shouted all over the place because I knew that the devil tried to take me out and he didn't succeed! Thank you Jesus that was all I could say, even when im making these stupid decisions you showed me your grace and mercy and covered me in your blood.

Chapter 6

New Surroundings

The shooting left me rattled and scared in ways I haven't felt since I was a small child, I literally felt like I had a target on my back and no one wanted to be around me because they thought they would come back and finish the job, so I felt like a marked woman I had this deep sadness like I made an irrevocable choice and now my sons would be orphans because they were going to lose their mother. I was depressed and I felt hopeless, I ended up back at my moms house and this added to my misery and she was going to find a way to use this situation against me. I had to get out of Reading once and for all I can't stay here I have to leave now and I kept hearing a very urgent GO in my spirit I couldn't trust anyone and I needed to start fresh, I had my income tax and I had my student loan money left over I was moving to Pottstown. I had a church family down there and this was far enough away from Reading but close enough to see my family so that was the move. In March of 2001 I made the move to Pottstown PA so I could start over and clear my head and life from all the bad decisions I had made back home. I found a cute 2 bedroom apartment and started my new life in Pottstown, the church blessed me with furniture and I found a job and things were looking up. See the problem with a geographical move is if your mind isn't renewed and you don't change your inner self you are bound to make the same mistakes. Paul says it best in Romans 7:15-18 For what I am doing I do not understand. For what I will do, that I do not practice; but what I hate that I do. If then, I do what I will not do, I agree with the law that it is good. But now it is no longer I who do it but the sin that dwells in me.

That sin was ever present in my life and just trying not to do something was not going to fix it I was fresh off the streets and even though I was in church I still had this thing about men and I didnt know how to just be alone and wait. I felt like I needed to fill my space up with people I didn't like being alone. That same spirit I couldn't stand in my mother I too had adopted, it was really a generational curse and a familiar spirit and all the women in my family had it. I didn't realize it then so I just thought that was just who I was. This is the number one Lie the enemy loves to tell us, especially women that that is just who we are." THE DEVIL IS A LIE" We have all power and dominion and we are able to be delivered from any and all Spirits that would seem to just be a character flaw it's actually something you can be delivered from. I would have loved to have all the information that I have right now, but i'm glad that I have what I need now so that I can help others that may have been in the same situation. As I continued on my journey in Pottstown I had a few sexual relationships and found myself in a relationship for a year this particular man was nice on the surface but that familiar spirit was real and it was following me. He spoke to all the insecurities in me, for the first time in my life I didn't feel beautiful, I didn't feel like I was as pretty as I actually was. This relationship spoke to every place in me that i thought was hidden, I was insecure of where I came from, of my family and the way I was brought up. I was second guessing every part of who I thought I was. I thought I was pretty, I thought I was a good person, this man told me to my face that he was leaving me because there was someone better for him. I couldn't even believe it! Who did he think he was? Did he know who I was? No the question really was did I know who I was? Did I see myself the way God saw me or did I see myself as this man saw me? I was broken, I sat up night after night crying myself to sleep because I came to the realization that I was exactly what this man said I was and I was destined to be just like my mother was. That couldn't have been farther from the truth but I didn't know that then. Now I'm going to stop and give some scriptures that speak to the identity of the children of the Most High God. We will always be able to fight against the opinions of others once we know who we are in Christ.

Genesis 1:27 So God created man in His own image of God He created him; male and female He created them.

Now if that scripture doesn't put in perspective who you are and how you were created let me give you one more.

Psalm 139:13-14 For you formed my inward parts; You covered me in my mother's womb. I will praise You, for I am fearfully and wonderfully made: marvelous are your works, and that my soul knows very well.

That is how I see myself now and I will never allow anyone's opinion of me or their own insecurity tell me who I'm not or what I can't have. I was in this place where I had to get back up and remember who I was and not allow these words spoken over me determine where I was able to go. The enemy was assaulting my character and my identity because as long as I thought small and didnt feel like I deserved anything he could hold me down.

Our relationship ended and I started on my quest to show him who I was for real, this was time for me to prove him wrong, I'm good at that my whole life people told me who I wasn't and what I couldn't be and do and I kept pushing past that and proving them wrong. So I got a job at a bank, enrolled in college and started fixing up my apartment, I was sad and broken but now I was angry so I was on the quest to get validation for everything he said that hurt me. I would invite certain guys over if they told me I was pretty, and made me feel better about myself. But none of them were for me. I didn't really want them. I had to prove something so I had to make sure he was looking if I was going to bring someone over. I had become the queen of petty and it wasn't cute or mature but this was who I was and how I thought at this stage in my life, so here we go. While in school I had an orientation class I was supposed to be in last semester but it was full so now it's January of 2003 and I'm in my second semester of college and I'm majoring in Registered nursing. So it's not a Pediatrician but I was derailed a bit so now I had to try for Pediatric nurse instead. I was excited, I loved to learn and I felt my strength coming back. I wasn't as sad and I didnt cry myself to sleep nearly as much anymore so I had my game face on and I was ready for my next chapter. I met this guy in my orientation class. He saves me a seat and has a pencil because although I'm adulting I still struggle in my life, I'm late and unprepared but I made it so that is half the battle, I showed up. He was a nice guy and very funny so I liked sitting next to him so that seat saving, became him picking me up for school so I wasn't late anymore. Like i said he was such a nice guy, almost too nice what does he really want? He would listen to all my crazy dating stories and we would laugh and I found myself as time progressed not really wanting to invite these random guys over, I looked forward to seeing him and just talking to him he became my friend. I never really had a friend like him, most of the time it's clear early that these guys want to sleep with me and usually I would sleep with them and get them out of my face so I could move on to the next, but he was different I didn't want to sleep with him I really just enjoyed his company, he would keep me company in the library as I was working on a paper. He started to wait for me after class and we would walk to our next class together and just talk. Months had passed by and we were still just being friendly. He was married and had 2 sons, one of which he would bring to my home and play with my son who at the time had just turned 3 they played well together. Whenever I needed him he was there, I started to feel myself falling for him and that was dangerous because like I said he was married, but what was this I was feeling? I was 25 years old and have never felt this way about anyone, not these types of feelings, although I loved my crush when I was a child at that time and didn't understand being in love. We would just have so much fun together and sometimes would talk on the phone for hours, he was the only one that would still listen to my ex boyfriend drama and just laugh.

I found myself getting sad when the weekend would come because then I wouldn't get to see him at school or talk to him on the phone as much. I needed this man in my life. I can't shake this feeling it was so strong and something unlike anything I ever felt. Well now today what that was was that same ole familiar spirit coming around again and this time He was planning to wreak havoc in my life to have to sink back into that depressive state, but this time is masqueraded as something sweet and innocent but under all this something was brewing and it would change the course of my life forever.

Chapter 7

The affair

It was a cool crisp day in September. It was the end of summer and fall was knocking on the door but it was still dress weather. This particular day we didnt have class but I had an appointment and my friend offered to take me, so we took the 30 minute drive to Norristown and talked and laughed the whole time in the car. I had this nagging feeling in my chest I had to get off how I felt, I had to tell this man that I had now fallen in love with him. I needed him, I loved him and I wanted him. But how do I tell this married man all this, he will reject me and I will be so embarrassed and hurt. Maybe I shouldn't. I will just keep it to myself and play Erykah Badu's Next Lifetime in my head and keep moving. But that pull was strong so i broke the ice and I told him how I felt and much to my surprise he felt the same way too! Now normally I would have thought he was just another married man that wanted some pretty young stuff no bigs been here before. This was different though he had a look in his eye I never seen before, this man knew everything about me and never judged me once. We shared crazy family stories and he knew things about me that no one else knew I felt safe with him. As crazy as this sounds I felt like I could trust him with my heart, he had been so gentle and sweet with me and told me all the time how beautiful I was and that made me feel good and special. I started to feel like if this man was really married he wouldn't feel like this about me.

Im hearing I wish playing in my head its 2003 and this is now my life I know he has a wife and kids but I wish I would have never met him because even when I win someone has to lose and I didn't want that I really didn't but I couldn't help but feel like I needed this in my life I was 25 and I was so broken i didn't even know why I was doing this.

Clearly I'm spending more time with him than his wife so obviously I have something she doesn't. This is how broken women validate themselves. I was a perfect example of that and I needed to take timeout to speak to that level of brokenness, see I was still hurting from the damage the last guy did, he deconstructed everything I thought about myself and this married man was building it back up. Or so I thought but the man that builds his house on the sand that house can not stand the winds and the ocean because the moment that tide comes out and the waves start crashing against it then it will fall. So at this point we were both ready to start this affair. He came back to my apartment that day and we did things that I had only dreamed about doing with him. It was crazy and fulfilling and wild and ultimately it was a soul tie that I was creating. I was joining myself with this man in such a way that not only did he have my body but he had my mind, my heart and my soul. This was a dangerous place to be because I may have slept around but they never got my heart or my mind most of them I didn't even remember, but this guy he had every part of me and I was in deep. He groomed me for 9 months just being sweet and nice and showing me what I needed to see in a man. He was smart, cunning the worst kind of predator. He zeros in on the place in you that is the most vulnerable and then exploits it for his own personal gain. It wasn't hard to get me to fall in love with him, all he had to do was placate that broken little girl that needed to feel the safety of a father and he got me hook line and sinker. We spent every single day we could spend together as much as we could and then came our first drill weekend. Let me explain drill weekend. He was in the military and had a weekend drill once a month and he would lie to his wife and say he was going to be with his sisters and then he would be sleeping at my house. We had the best time and that weekend if I already wasn't in love. I was in even deeper now. I literally cried while we made love. I have never in my life felt like that, what is happening? Now was I torn still of course, that part of me that still knew the Lord and what He says about this kind of stuff had me wanting to back out and go my separate ways. That heart of mine though is really deceitful and it betrayed me every time I had the nerve to do it. I saw him out in the streets and he acted like he had never seen me before, I was so confused I didn't know how it worked in this affair world. I hadn't had an affair to this degree and I didnt want to be ignored. How could he? Now the question was how could I, How could I be this broken that I was allowing myself to settle for half of something and this really spoke to my bad decision making and that I was lacking so much in my life that I actually felt like this was the best I was ever treated.

Don't get me wrong, he was a professional womanizer and was very good at what he did, when we were together he made me feel like I was the only woman in the world, I felt like the most beautiful, the sexiest and the most amazing person on the planet when I was with him. Now all these feelings though valid were temporary because once he went back to his wife I no longer existed in his world. That is when the reality of the danger of what I had gotten myself into was evident to me. My heart would literally get ripped out every other day and he kept coming back and putting a bandaid on it and I was right back in waiting for my turn, like a slow running kid at recess waiting to be picked for tag. It was sickening, I was so ashamed of myself I knew better, I wasnt this weak woman that allowed a man to have this type of control over them. I was different, I loved them and left them. I was the heartbreaker. I didn't get my heartbroken right? That wasn't who I was, or was it? My heart was so broken that I don't know how I was still standing. I had literally jumped from the frying pan into the fire. At least the last guy wasn't married, and although painful he was honest with me he still hurt me but it wasn't the same, he never pretended to be so in love with me that he couldn't be without me and then walked past me in the street like I was a stranger. Now that he never did, I'm trying so hard to lift myself out of this despair. The feelings of not being good enough are creeping in again. We are now in the throws of an all out affair I mean it's hot and heavy, so much so that we lived around the corner from one another someone was bound to see us and rat us out the town was small people were nosy and I became a target, and it wasn't long until his wife was knocking on my door.

Well it's time to face it. We knew it would happen eventually so there she is. I'm staring at this short, pasty white woman that looks distraught but also not surprised, she asked if her husband was there. So I told her if you wait a few you may be able to catch him because he is coming back. So sure enough he pulled around the corner and we were standing outside. I looked at him, and he looked at me and then her and she asked the fatal question " Are you in love with Her?" He looked her in the eye and told her yes I am, I'm in love with her and I stood there with this smile on my face as if I won some prize or something, like this was some sort of ultimate validation like I was receiving the Oscar of the side chick award and i'm ready to make my acceptance speech. I was literally standing there feeling like yes maybe now he will be with me and only me. It's out in the open we don't have to hide or sneak around he will love me now and be everything I have always wanted someone to be. She left and he went after her, I didn't understand what was happening, I did hear him say he was in love with me, so what was the problem? He came back that night and spent the night with me and woke up the next morning made me breakfast and we had such a good time we never even talked about what happened and we actually started to just laugh at this poor woman's expense. This would be a long line of times that his wife would catch us together. We even had the audacity to go to church together and sit up in there like a married couple until she walked in. We turned around and all she said was "What's going on here" We just looked at each other and grinned and walked outside because now she is making a scene. She started talking about me and saying some nasty things and of course she had the right but back then you weren't just going to say anything to me and now im about to fight this lady in the parking lot I was just out of control, we were out of control and this is what happens when you allow your emotions to make decisions nothing is ever rational. The demonic possession in my life was real, that soul tie I created was deep and it was going to be a wild road before it was broken. To keep this story short we kept seeing each other even though he went back home, I then gave him an ultimatum and wanted him to leave and he wouldn't so I left and moved 4 hrs away to Chester VA its now 2004 and I couldn't take it anymore and needed a change once again I thought changing my geographical location was going to change the situation for me. My heart was sick, I was so in love and my heart was so broken it didn't matter where I went I was still going to feel the way I did. The only thing that would fix that would be to completely surrender my heart to the

Lord and let him heal me. But I wasn't ready for that. I didn't trust God yet enough to allow him to take over my life. Even though I moved all the way to VA he was still a part of my life, I couldn't shake him, I was sad and miserable in VA and was so homesick. When he came to visit me I was excited and sad all at the same time happy to see him but sad because I know he couldn't stay. I was literally torturing myself and it was with my own choices. I then invited him down after I was settled and doing better there, had a job, a cute place and was in the process of buying a car. I was definitely doing my best. But I missed him more than I could ever admit, my heart longed for him, my body craved him. I just missed him and I tried to be with other guys and all that did was make me think more about him so he came to VA. He stayed with me for 2 weeks and told me he was going to go back and get the rest of his things and promised to come back, he just wanted to be with me. I waited no call or anything weeks went by and he never came back, he didn't even have the decency to say hey this 2 weeks was fun but I won't be back, be a man about it at least I would have known where I stood. Now I know what you're thinking, why would she even allow this after everything he put her through? This heart I have always held out hope that one of these times he really would be with me. I'm telling you this heart was deceitful and it was betraying my good sense everytime I turned around. But unlike a traditional affair we were in love and the rules were a bit different for us I could see the love in his eyes when he looked at me but what I didn't realize then is that he was broken too and didn't really know how to love anyone completely. The only woman that he truly loved he lost when he was 18, his mother and later on God would allow me to see why he would just leave a string of broken hearts in his wake. I allowed this man to break my heart again, why did I ever think he would do anything but keep going back? He was bound by obligation and at the time had a young son and no matter what he would tell me I think he really did love his wife. I told myself he didnt love me, he loved who I was to him, he loved how I made him feel but me stripped down and raw, he didnt love me. He couldn't see my pain and actually truly love me and that was a hard pill to swallow, once again my self esteem took a hit, because I was prettier than this woman, I was better for him I thought I just felt like I wasn't good enough, I just didn't have enough money, didn't come from the right family or whatever. I allowed that inferiority complex to creep back in. This feeling was deeply rooted and these men just fed it, they didn't create it. I was born into rejection and inferiority so this is why I attracted people that saw me like that because that is how I saw myself. The facts and the truth were contradictory in my life. I would be haunted by the love I felt for this man and I would allow him to use me and emotionally abuse me for years and even though I wasn't with him he never left my heart, in my mind it was just terrible timing and I would hold a torch for this man, and I will be in love with him for the rest of my life I thought and nothing would take it away. This would of been a great place to just stop everything in my life and allow God to heal my heart and take control, I was going to church and I believed I just didn't think that God could take care of me in this area I believed the lie the devil told me that this was my consequence for being with someone's husband I would never have anyone that would love me and see me and the one man in my life that actually did was committed to someone else so I was just doomed to a fate of relational mediocrity. "THE DEVIL IS A LIAR" I should have asked God to fix it to make me better or to help my unbelief. I just prayed for the pain to stop, it was unlike anything I had ever felt no one should ever have to endure that type of pain and anguish in their heart and torment in their mind God is a healer, He is a restorer He can stop the pain all you have to do is ask and I endured so much unnecessary pain because I never gave it to God completely and I felt like Jeremiah in this passage. Jeremiah 15:18-19 says "Why is my pain perpetual and my wound incurable, which refuses to be healed? Will you surely be to me like an unreliable stream, as waters fail? Even as Jeremiah asked God the hard question of will this be it Lord is this just how my life will be? I allowed my emotions to dictate my actions and it only became worse from here.

Chapter 8

The marriage

I was trying to move on and get my life back on track, I started going to school. I got a settlement check and was able to furnish my house and I even had my job right in walking distance to my home. I could see God at work in my life. I was still in a lot of emotional pain and would cry myself to sleep almost every night. I became bitter and resentful and I wanted him to hurt like I was hurting. Once again my mind wasn't rational and I was allowing my emotions to dictate the choices I was making. Emotional instability+Irrational Thinking=DISASTER

So after this last blow I decided to be petty and immature and said well if he can be married then I can as well and I grabbed the first man who smiled at me and made me giggle and brought him into my brokenness and actually married him! It was the worst 3 months of my life and everything I had built in my life up to that point having this man in my life single handedly dismantled it all. Now I want to clarify one thing: I do not blame anyone for any of the things that have happened in my adult life. I made these terrible decisions outside of the will of God and I suffered the consequences of each decision that I have made. This man after 3 months just became more of a burden and I realized I made a mistake, I had created one fine mess in my life, this man never loved me and I surely wasn't in love with him, I couldn't have just shacked up with him like normal folks nope I had to get all churchy and say hey since your not doing anything and i'm not either how about we have ourselves a little wedding! This is when my crazy goes to a whole other level and I really needed Jesus because I was extremely impulsive. I never prayed about this union, I sure didn't have confirmation and I had the nerve to drag this man into a premarital counseling session and still married him. God was giving me all the signs not to do this and me and all my bullheaded stubbornness kept moving. I was a decision making bull in an emotional china shop just a wake of disaster behind me. My sister called me a few days before and said are you sure you want to do this? My first out. Then I couldn't find the church on the wedding day and was an hour late. I could have done the runaway bride thing but nope kept going! Out number two. Then on the night before my wedding I went to see a friend and he gave me a bottle of vodka and said you need this more than me, I don't even drink but did that night my first time being drunk. Now I will say pressure from the church and the guilt they put on you when you are living with someone even if your not sure if that is your person they will push you into marrying them. This is why the divorce rate is so high in the church so many people in general young and old trying not to commit sexual sin, that they rush to get married and do not even know who they are marrying or why they are marrying them, they are both broken and horny and once the sexual excitement wears off then they realize they made the biggest mistake of their lives and now they have to go through the painful task of trying to disconnect yourself from someone you never were supposed to be with anyway. Later on in the book I will talk about Kingdom relationships and once you are living in your state of wholeness you will attract Gods pick for your life. Now one of my gifts is being an extremist once I put my mind to something I see it through until the end. In this case I used my gift for evil and not good and it felt like I was having an outer body experience like someone else was marrying him. I sure did see this all the way to the altar and immediately had buyers remorse and it was almost like I can see my angels shaking their heads but what I love about my Heavenly Father is even when we make the worst choices he finds us a way out, now it may not have been the easiest way out but it was a way out nonetheless. So now im planning my escape because I was just miserable, well I thought being able to have sex without asking for forgiveness was going to be fun, after the first 3 days I was over it and him.

We had a lot of arguments and I started to see his real personality and character coming to the surface. But who am I kidding I started looking for a way out from the moment I said I DO. He didn't want to exit my life quietly and decided once he found out I was about to leave him and I was pregnant, he decided he was going to put his hands on me and that is one thing I would not tolerate under any circumstances after what I saw my mother go through. He pushed me and held me hostage in that room and I lost it and he got all in my face and had me backed in a corner trying to invoke fear, as he continued to threaten me I begged him to let me go to the bathroom but he wouldn't let up, he was going to tell me all the things he hated about me at this moment and I was going to listen. I was so upset, and angry and trying to not punch this dude right in his funky breath mouth, as he was spitting and yelling in my face all I could do was think of my baby. I just stood there crying and pleading for the bathroom and my son who was 5 at the time came running up the steps to see if I was ok and then and only then did he let me out of that room. I had instant flashbacks of that moment at 9 years old when. My mother's husband held us hostage and I ran as fast as I could out of that house and into the car, I didn't trust him and a man that has nothing to lose when he is about to lose everything is very dangerous. I almost lost my baby that night after this ordeal started having pain in my stomach and went to the hospital and was hooked up to IVs and just prayed that God would keep my baby safe. At this point I was probably about 6 to 7 weeks pregnant so it was easy to miscarry in the early stages. After hours in the hospital, the baby was fine and I could be released and I went right to the Magistrate and pressed charges against him. Didn't know what in the Mayberry was going on here and why I had to go through all these hoops to get this man arrested but I will find out how battered women are treated in the good old state of VA. I sat there and thought great now I'm going to be connected to this clown for the rest of my life. What have I done? I would find out quickly he had no interest in being a father to my daughter. He just wanted the option but didn't really want to do anything so he was just as much of a ghost as the other 2 so I had nothing to worry about.

Chapter 9

Transitions

It was the hardest period of my life. I had lost my home and I was now trying to figure out my next move. So of course Mr Married man was right there offering his support, came to see me in VA and then when everything came to a head with this fake husband, I ended up in a domestic violence shelter because they never took the keys from this weirdo and he was out of jail. I had nowhere to go so of course Mr Married Man would urge me to come back to PA where I had a bigger support system, or so I thought. I had to move all my things out of this house and put it in storage until my next move. I did get storage but one of my friends so graciously said," Hey, I have an empty trailer and i'm not moving into it yet you can store your stuff there for free so you don't have to worry. I should have never agreed to that one it would later turn into, "Oh, by the way, I lost my trailer and all of your things inside". What she really meant to say was thank you for letting me hook my trailer up with all your fly furniture because you were just swindled and I was never your friend. I was furious and in one fell swoop lost every single earthly possession including pictures of my kids as babies. My friend had to talk me out of going down there and giving this lady the beatdown of her life. I couldn't believe this was happening but this was just the beginning of what would unfold once I stepped foot back in that God forsaken place I was so desperate to leave. I had so much anger, frustration and disappointment building. I was a ticking time bomb and now my emotions are even more scattered and heightened because I was pregnant. Any thoughts I had of going back to Virginia diminished even though I did look at an apt and was set to start classes for my RN in the fall and even received glowing recommendations from my teachers at the tech school I was attending, where I had ultimately met the fake husband. After this fiasco I think I'm done with VA. Here I am pregnant and homeless. I got back to PA and none of my family helped me. They never really did. My mom offered to keep my sons but I was going to have to find somewhere else to go. What kind of hand that rocks the cradle type of stuff is that? My kids can stay but your pregnant daughter is on her own! No worries mother, I really didn't want to stay with her. I didn't need that stress on top of everything else I had to deal with. So I had people that weren't my family but treated me as such that opened their homes to me and helped me transition from one of the most stressful parts of my life.

So now I left this deadbeat husband and after the whole physical assault business I was all done with him had him arrested and had a protective order against him. I will protect my baby and my children at all costs. They had been through enough. I had moved them all over the place and my decisions have cost them once again. I didn't see at the time that I was doing the exact thing that my mother did to me. I put my physical needs over the health and emotional welfare of my children and I felt terrible about that and I just wanted to protect them and do better from now on. Now here I am back in the same place I had left 1 yr prior, I just wanted peace but the way my life was set up all I became was an agent of chaos everything I touched became full of drama. Of course myself and Mr Married Man we are back to the same old shenanigans sneaking and meeting and doing what we do and at this point I really didn't have any fight left about that situation. I just accepted what he gave me and tried to keep my anger under control. I would have a run in with his wife at a football practice I was attending with my roommate's son. I saw her coming my way and my first thought was that maybe she was walking to someone else because I know she isn't crazy enough to come confront me at these kids practice. Like I said earlier I was a ticking time bomb way too much was happening and I just wasn't in the mood for this lady, so although yes I was still sleeping with her husband she was still with him after she knew he was in love with me so I felt at this point you deserve what you get. I know my mentality at that point was my predelieverance days and I meant that and told her exactly what I thought of her and the situation. She had the audacity to come over to me and start talking crazy, this belly was fooling folks and I had to tell her about herself because now wasn't the time and I wasn't the one. I had some very colorful things to say to her on that field and needless to say the coaches no longer wanted me to come to the practices. Even though she walked up to me I was minding my business and wasn't even there for Mr Married man didn't even know he would be there and honestly as shady as he was he wouldn't have talked to me anyway and I was not in the business of embarrassing myself. This had become a regular occurrence with this lady because she just couldn't believe that I wasn't pregnant from her husband and no matter how many times I told her that she still felt the need to come for me. The last straw was on my way dropping off my roommate. We drove down his street, ok yes I may or may not have been checking the scenery. She happened to be outside at the time and put her arms out as if to say what's up, like she wanted to fight. Now I'm at the end of the block and I put that car in reverse and proceeded to back up that block, all I kept hearing was my roommate yelling Nooooo, keep going and I looked at her and drove away. After these latest incidents I felt the need to protect myself and my daughter, so I went to the police station and explained to them what was happening. Now I wasn't scared by any means I just wanted to get the word out that this woman was provoking me and regardless of the circumstances I was pregnant and wanted to protect myself and my child. Of course Mr Married man was smack in the middle of this chaos and honestly I think it excited him in such a way that he had these women ultimately fighting over him. Now I wasn't directly fighting over him but I was fighting for my own defense and I was already angry and frustrated and wanted someone to take it out on. I felt like she was living my life, while me and my kids were displaced. This chick was still enjoying her home and her children and her perfect little family. What did I have for all my troubles? Nothing but heartache, I was angry, frustrated and honestly I was lonely and afraid I just wanted things to make sense again.

It was the year 2005 Katrina had hit New Orleans on the same day I lost everything I owned it was quite the year, One of my favorite songs at the time was Let me Hold you by Bow Wow and Omarion and I was longing for a man to show me this type of love, sitting in my car at the park just listening to the radio and thinking about my life and what was happening in it and something had to change. I knew what I really wanted because I was a hopeless romantic. I just didn't think I deserved it. I had done too much and went too far, so I just sat in my car and started to cry. I definitely knew Mr Married man wasn't going to give it to me and I had to get that out of my head. I have been all over this state trying to find a place to go and no one could house us. I didn't know what was happening but it may be time for another move my kids are now 9 and 5. I was really trying to deal with all this emotional trauma and still be a parent and each day it was harder and harder. So much was coming at me from every angle and I just needed to get away from all this chaos that was surrounding me. I was working with a case manager from the local domestic violence center and she helped me find a shelter and it was in Maryland. I didn't know how this was all going to work out. I just knew being in PA wasn't working out. I wasn't going back to VA and I couldn't stay here. The enemy lured me back there with false promises, when I really needed that man he wasn't anywhere to be found, gas was so high that summer and I had literally ran out of gas on my way to meet him and he never answered his phone. Strangers and one of my friends helped me get back on the road. So that was it. I was moving to Maryland. I didn't know a soul there but I knew that God was opening this door I could feel it. I wasn't about to stay here and deal with anymore nonsense everything was telling me to go. So I got everything together my friend and her husband filled up my tank and got me a new battery and I was all packed and ready to go. We left PA on Oct 3 which was my son's 10th birthday so I felt like I was giving my kids the gift of starting over and this time I was determined not to make the same choices. I gave that place one last look. I let Mr. Married man know I was leaving and we were off once again.

Chapter 10

A New Beginning

So we arrived at the shelter a few hours later and this would begin a journey in my life that would strengthen me and stretch my faith in what God is able to do when you just believe that he can make ways out of no way. If I tell you it was all sunshine and rainbows after all that i would be telling a great lie. It was a difficult transition. We had never been to a shelter before we had a curfew and we all had to share the same room but I would do my best to make it as comfortable a transition as possible. At this point I was about 5 months pregnant and couldn't really work so I was going to do my best to keep myself busy and become acclimated with my new surroundings. Although I was still walking around with this broken heart I still would keep a smile on my face no one would ever be able to see what I was going through. I was very lonely and sad and once the kids were asleep I would just talk to God and cry. I just wanted to know what it felt like to go through a pregnancy with someone that actually stayed and did all those sweet and loving things with. I longed for every child I had. I was alone, no one was there to go to lamaze classes or any of the fun stuff that couples do when they have a baby. I watched way too many TLC shows and dreamed of having that one day, but this wasn't the time and this was not that day. I was in a new city with just myself and my boys trying to jumpstart my life. One thing that I had in me was a can't quit attitude, no matter how hard it became I knew that a better day was coming. So we are getting settled in the shelter. I found a church and started to regularly attend. I honestly started to feel some relief, I enrolled in college and was making the most of this situation. I still had the car so that was a step up from most of the other residents so I would give people rides if they needed and they would pay me and this was a blessing to me because I needed gas most of the time so God knew. I was able to get my first refund check a few weeks after school started and I was able to take me and the kids shopping. I had lost everything so as winter fast approached I had no winter clothes and my boys didn't either. I spent as much time doing fun stuff with my boys as I could, I felt like I had to compensate because I felt guilty about what we were going through. So to take their mind off we would do laser tag, go to the Baltimore Aquarium, hit the movies or anything else they wanted to do. I enjoyed spending time with my kids. This is just what I needed time for just myself and my boys. This was the first time in a while that I didn't have a man in my life, now I had a few guys that I was seeing but nothing major, I still had this Married man heart issue that only God could heal and he was waiting patiently for me to just give it to him. Now I have been in Baltimore now for a few months and time was coming for this baby to come. I had found a Dr and was going to have my daughter at the Franklin Square Hospital in Essex Maryland. It became difficult to sleep because I was so big and my younger son was always acting up knowing I really couldn't chase him or spank him, he played me like a fiddle. It was a normal night. I went to sleep. I could feel some discomfort in my stomach but I didn't think much of it, didn't think I was in labor because honestly I didn't know what it felt like to go into labor naturally because I was induced and overdue both times. I was in labor and didn't realize it so I drank a soda and went to sleep, this little girl had to have a sprite every night. It was crazy the cravings I had while I was pregnant. I would literally drive back to Reading to get Burritos because I had such a strong craving and I wasn't very hungry all during this pregnancy and actually lost more weight than I gained. I had to drink Ensure take iron pills because I became anemic as well. I'm sure all the stress I was under didnt help in the beginning. This time went by so fast I'm actually going to miss being pregnant feeling my baby inside of me and knowing that I get to keep her protected from a world that would hurt her and break her heart. I didn't mind keeping her in there a little longer, but she had other plans. I woke up in the middle of the night because I thought I was peeing myself. I went to look and apparently I'm leaking amniotic fluid. She was due the next day so honestly she was right on time. So I take my time completely calmly. I shower get dressed, pack clothes for the boys and pack myself a bag for the hospital and nonchalantly knock on my neighbors door at the shelter. She opened the door and I said "So I may or may not be in labor so if you want to drive with me cool" She was like what! Oh my goodness we have to go now! I just laughed and said I'm driving. I knew how my uterus was set up and this child would not be coming out on its own, every child I had I had to be induced both my boys were late 15 days and 7 days so this was nothing new. So I call my Dulla which is what they appointed me with at the hospital so I wouldn't be completely alone. They let my boys stay in the room and I had to get pitocin because i wasn't dilated but my water broke and she had to come so I started the labor process no meds just a little pain meds to take the edge off they upped the pitocin and it was on, my contractions were coming fast and the baby's heart rate was dropping. What was happening this wasn't a part of the plan, this never happened before they needed to get her out now! I started to push and before I knew it, she slid out. But wait why don't I hear anything? Why isn't my baby crying? She was blue and they took her from me right away. I couldn't even hold her. They put her cute little body under that light and got her breathing. Thank God I was so worried I couldn't wait to give her sweet little face a bunch of kisses. The married man said he would be in the room with me when I had her, he knew how important that was to me. I knew that she wasn't his but it would have been nice to just have him there with me holding my hand.

But he wasn't and I honestly haven't heard from him in quite a while. I'm sure he was being a good husband with me out of the picture is what I thought to myself. So it was just me and babygirl, this was an all too familiar scenario of myself and my own mother just 29 years ago, my sister had come to pick up my boys and see the baby and my mom and my best friend had come as well, it was nice to see familiar faces. Especially at this time but after everyone had left it was just me and my baby she didn't go into the nursery much I kept her with me. I sat there alone in my hospital room just thinking about my life and how thankful I was that she was healthy. It was time for discharge and the nurse asked me if anyone was coming to pick me up, I said no I drove it's just me. She kind of looked at me with this sympathetic look on her face and I just smiled and said it's alright I'm used to this. I got the baby ready to go. I had a hard time fighting back the tears when I saw all the other moms being wheeled down by their partners and all the family that was with them. Meanwhile I was driving myself out of there and taking my newborn daughter back to a homeless shelter. This was a very sobering situation. I was smacked with the realization that I was utterly alone for the 3rd time I was going to be doing this alone. I never understood how I could pick this bad every time but what I now know is when your brokenness is doing the picking this is what happens. Even though I know I was physically alone at this time I knew that God was with me throughout my entire life, His word says that he would never leave me nor forsake me and each situation I found myself in He was always there to pick me up and that was all I knew.

Now a single mother to three kids it was time to start making better decisions I do not want my daughter to ever think that it is ok to allow a man to mistreat you and break your heart, I want her to learn better I want to break this generational curse in my family it will stop with me I want to be the best mother I can be. Months go by and low and behold Mr. Married man is still alive and decides to call me isn't that nice. I could feel that anger and hurt rising up again at the sound of his voice, where have you been? What have you been doing? Why haven't I heard from you? I had all these questions in my head but instead I played it cool and just said oh hey nice of you to finally call me. At this time I was out of the shelter and in transitional housing and me and the kids had an efficiency that we shared so it was better than the shelter, and it felt a little bit more like home. God had worked miracles for me during my time in MD strangers were opening their homes and ways were being made. I had a job at the school and the kids were doing well. I actually liked MD the time there really gave me a chance to be who I needed to be for my kids, now trust me it wasn't all rosy we had some struggles my boys were both having behavior issues and I was trying to deal with all of that on top of a new baby, school and still dealing with this heart issue. Now i started to notice a pattern here with Mr married man and im getting most of this insight as I write this book whenever I really needed him and was in a desperate situation he would conveniently do his famous disappearing act. Then he would show back up on the scene when he felt like the coast was clear and maybe I would be settled enough to want to engage back into this affair because trust me if there was one thing that we did well it was in the bedroom and i'm sure that is what had him coming back time and time again, now he would beg to differ if asked that question but I know the truth. So he comes back with the same old sweet talk, and because I'm just a fool for him I fall for it, and he caught me at a time when I was just missing him and seeing him even if it's briefly I was down for it. I still held on to this fantasy that we could be who we were when we first met that I could reach the heights of ecstasy with him as we once did. Like an addict I was chasing a feeling that would never again return, the circumstances surrounding us will never be the same, but the broken part of me kept hoping that one day things would be different. I just knew if we could just be together and have a real chance of being a couple that everything would be great. My kids loved him and trusted him and despite all his foolishness he was an excellent father. It was now 2006 and 3 yrs have passed since the beginning of this affair, the day that man walked into my life I was never the same. So I let him back in and we started seeing each other. I'm going to PA and he is coming to MD. I was like ok maybe this is what he needed me to be gone for a while to really show you what you miss most about me. This was going nowhere fast and I was so in love that I was about to uproot my life once again. Let me take a moment here to talk about the dangers of not knowing who we are in Christ. We will allow every dead situation to attach itself to us and drain us of any strength and happiness we were trying to facilitate in our lives. We will accept things that will never measure up to the blessings God wants to give us in our lives. We literally forfeit our destiny by looking at our history and allowing it to define us instead of God's word and purpose for our lives.

Chapter 11

Making moves

So at this point I'm still in MD living my best life and trying to still deal with this heart issue that has gripped me in such a way I keep falling for the Okie Doke. Now what I didn't know then that I know now is this heart issue is actually a soul tie I created with this man that would follow me for close to 15 yrs but let me not get ahead of myself because there is still so much story to tell. So now it's still 2006 my daughter is about 3 months old and I'm working and still going to school. One beautiful Spring day as I was going to Target with my neighbor. I met this extremely handsome man, that I will call my time filler, he was sweet and kind and just happened to be driving a convertible Benz. Now we exchanged numbers and it was on that I started to talk to him nightly and he was definitely taking my mind off of Mr. Married Man so this was a welcome distraction. I knew it was not anything major, but he made me feel desired and I could trick my mind into believing that he could be the one. My brokenness was still in full effect and I just needed to feel wanted and loved and I didn't care where it came from. Don't get me wrong on paper this man was an ideal catch, he was handsome, financially stable, had a beautiful home and a few cars he was set but something was missing he just seemed very emotionally unavailable.

Not that I was, I still had this little heart issue I refused to deal with so I was really no better. We start seeing each other which basically was just for sex, and conversation I really didn't have interest or the mental capacity for anything else I was basically just lonely and he was filling my time. Now trust me Mr Married Man can smell when I'm moving on because out the Blue here he comes with the same old tired lines I've been listening too for the past 3 years. I was just all over the place because at this time in my life I was also experimenting with women knowing dang gone well this was not even the way this should be going, but once again I refused to deal with this heart issue and it just had me making one poor decision after another. I have tried the whole girl on girl sex experience because Mr Married Man encouraged it and thought it was cute and sexy and even bought me some Lesbian porn so he didn't mind it obviously excited him. Like I explained before this man's presence in my life would change everything for me in more ways than one and none of it was good this wasn't just a soul tie this man was hooked into my heart with a fishhook type hold it's crazy. I will pause for a second and explain what this type of soul tie this is. The type of Soul Tie that was connected to myself and this man was a Hook and Barb which naturally would resemble a fish hook and in the spirit is a very dangerous oppression because it will take well over a decade for me to rid myself of this particular soul tie. I was just sick and despondent and couldn't really get myself together. I kept falling into this same snare and trap the enemy was laying for me. The fact that we were committing adultry and fornicating just made it worse. So now it's 2007 and I'm still somewhat seeing my time filler but I really just want to be with Mr. Married Man so here I go again. So now I'm talking about being with this simple dude again and decide to move to Delaware to be closer to him. This is when if this was a text I would just insert an eye rolling emoji because I was so sick of myself. So in April of 2007 we start the move to Delaware our apartment was done and we moved in April 9, 2007 so I'm trying to start over once again, my theme song "I can love you" by Mary J plays in my head while I'm trying to figure out why this man just doesn't want to be with me. Once again I'm just playing myself and continuing to add more hurt and pain into my life. This move though would prove to be a much better move and I will dig my roots in and spend a significant amount of time here. This is what I would like to say was me and My Married Man's swan song but it just got extremely weird. So in September of 2007 which will be exactly 4 years from our first sexual encounter. I was just tired he made way to many empty promises and I was exhausted and I really think he was as well he just wouldn't admit it. So I had met this chick at work a few months prior and I really started liking the attention she was giving me and she was what they would call in the gay world a stud which basically meant she was a very dominant female that wore men's clothes. This was all new to me because I was only attracted to feminine females but something about her was intriguing and for the first time in 4 yrs I wasn't thinking about Mr. Married Man so this may be a thing who knew.

Chapter 12

The Turning of Tides

I have officially broken up with Mr Married Man. It wasn't easy trust me. I bawled my eyes out for 2 hrs while I talked to him. It was a necessary talk but it was difficult for me because it was the end of an era, the Married Man saga was coming to an end and it was sad. Now you would think that I would now spend this time healing, giving my heart to the Lord completely and allowing the Holy Spirit to break this soul tie. But nope I still wasn't ready so what do I do? I start seeing this woman, who by the way has a girlfriend so yes my saga continues. Here is where I would put the hand on my face emoji if this was a text because I'm just a hot mess at this point and I keep doing the roll over situationships. I'm not going to lie, I definitely enjoyed the time I spent with my Bball Queen. This was a whole new experience. We had great chemistry, and she made me laugh.

She was a welcome distraction but it felt different because I really wasn't thinking about Mr Married Man anymore he became a painfully distant memory. Even though he kept trying to show up and make his presence known just because I didn't want him anymore, his selfish behind had to come and disrupt my life. This happened a few times until I really shut him all the way down. Now my B-ball Queen was a piece of work too. She was clearly cheating but she also spent more time with me than her girlfriend. She was enjoying my company as much as I was enjoying hers.

We went out on dates, we were literally best friends with benefits and although I was enjoying this because it was different I was still very much broken, hurting and lonely and this situationship will not improve my situation it will start a dangerous downward spiral in my life. One ratchet choice after the other I know my angels were sick of me. I was keeping my angels busy just not in a good way, they were protecting me and keeping me safe but all the things God wanted to do for me I had put on hold because I just would not deal with this heart issue I felt like out of sight is out of mind but that wasn't even the case I will hold on to Mr. Married Man and although I was no longer seeing him these feelings will lay dormant in my life and they will come up again just wait. So it's now the later part of 2007 and the BBall Queen and I are just having a ball, we are hanging out and just living our best lives. I'm enjoying myself but I'm still hurting because I ended up in a similar situation. Although she isn't married she is with this woman and they are living together and have been together at this point for 6 yrs so she is deeply rooted in love and emotions with this woman. We went out a lot though because her girlfriend was only 19 or 20 and couldn't go out to the clubs or bars and at the time I was 29 and she was 26 so it was on. I started to really get emotionally attached to her as well and became very sad when she wasn't around or when she had to go home because I enjoyed her company. Now this brokenness that has just become a part of my life just allowed me to basically jump from the frying pan into the fire. Never healing and never making healthy decisions this woman wasn't supposed to be anything more than my friend but my brokenness and I'm sure the lack of attention she was receiving just ushered us right into this affair. This went on for a few months and then B-ball Queen found out that this woman was cheating on her and it became a pure reality show. Of course I was right in the middle of it all, this is that agent of chaos syndrome kicking in again these familiar spirits just sought me out and my brokenness and the sin in my life just opened the door for them. So ultimately I thought I was in love with this woman and when she found out she was being cheated on I was right there to pick up the pieces and be that nurturer that I am even though I'm still hurt and broken myself but I will be that rider that I am and make sure the person in my life is doing well even if I'm not. So after the whole cheating fiasco we started dating a little more seriously but I don't think she could get over what happened and I know she missed her ex and wanted to be with her still and all I was in her life was a distraction. So ultimately we fooled around for about a yr and then in Aug of 2008 we ended our situationship. We took a trip together to LA which was my first time on the West Coast and I was excited because I felt like this could be a turning point in our lives but this was just the beginning of the end and after that trip I knew we were done and I still tried to be there for her but I couldn't. I was still dealing with my heart issue, my brokenness and those feelings of inadequacy that kept creeping in. Now let me pause to say my whole life I never felt good enough and I kept attracting those situations in my life that were showing me that I was not enough because of the brokenness in their lives that would drive them to treat others and themselves the way they had been. So I could not see how amazing I was and I kept sinking deeper into this oppressive and depressive state. Now once again I was dealing with not having a place to go because I started staying with BBall Queens mom so it was quite awkward once I no longer was with her and it just got weird in a lot of ways and it was best that I sever these ties with everyone so I can move on and so can they. Now at the time I was working at a 24 hr restaurant serving and this chick and her family came up there to start some stuff because they claimed I owed them 250.00 well the truth was once I moved out I no longer was obligated to give anything and I was with the drama so if they wanted it they could get it no problem I was tired of everyone and the anger and frustration I had built up would have exploded in ways that would have landed me right in jail so I decided to get them removed and act professionally. The funny thing is we are friends now after all the shenanigans we made amends in 2010 and to this present day we are still friends our original intended purpose before I dragged her into a relationship with my broken self. So let me pause and say it is so dangerous to keep bringing people into your life that you already know are not truly for you. This is where I should have allowed God to heal my heart, and heal me so that I can attract the right type of healthy relationship and ultimately find my one true Soul Mate but not me I will once again bring someone else in the midst of the brokenness.

Chapter 13

Bad to The Worst

Here I am it is now August of 2008 and I'm just running around doing whatever I want my children were with my mother because I was literally working 2 jobs barely sleeping I worked at a daycare from 9-6 and then I turned around and went back to work from 9pm to 4am so I may have slept about 3 hrs a night if that I was exhausted and I couldn't really take care of my kids, try and find another place and still try to work it was just too much for me so I allowed my kids to stay with my mom for what was supposed to be for the summer. She had other plans and started collecting Cash assistance and Food Stamps and everything and was trying not to let me see them or even speak to them on the phone it was just too much. I really missed my children and not being able to see them or talk to them was taking a toll on me. I met a few friends during my days at the diner, that was definitely my Happy Place because I was able to be myself interact with people, be fun and make money as well so there was nothing like working overnights and I was a phenomenon because I took all the orders without ever writing anything down and never made one mistake. I started to know my customers by the food they ordered and not even their names. I was a beast with it! So I met my one friend and for privacy sake I will call her my club homie. We would go out and just have so much fun and with the state of my life as it was I needed someone like that in my life. I was renting a room from one of my friends at works mother and at first this was an ideal situation, I was barely there I worked over nights and then I slept most of the day never ate there or cooked because I ate at work or out so I literally slept, showered and washed my clothes there and nothing else. So one night me and my Club Homie decided to go to this club after we went to eat. The waitress at Friday's told us about it so we were like why not we were both single and I decided that on my day off from the restaurant I was going to have a good time. So we headed on over to the Club that I believe was called Goodnights the Dj was on point and the vibe was cool. So when I walk in the door the bouncer catches my eye she was tall, she had beautiful skin and her smile was amazing so I start low key flirting and as she was checking me for weapons I made a few jokes and the next thing I know I was hanging at this door talking to Top Flight security. My club homie was like excuse me I know we came in here together what are you doing? So I decided to go see what was going on inside and mingle a bit. I couldn't stay away from that door though this beautiful woman intrigued me and then she let me know that they had a Night for the Gay and Lesbian community on Sundays so I was like ok bet I'm there. So we exchanged numbers and then Sunday I decided to go check out the scene. It was a vibe but this community is small so there were definitely a lot of familiar faces in that place and I saw the ex who at this time I am not speaking too because she played herself and I'm not even the one. So she saw me and I'm just laughing and chatting with my Top Flight Security and she was like let me know if she tries to start with you I will kick her and the whole crew out. We don't do that here. I was like yes look at my baby looking out for me already. Now let me just say this woman would be a very significant part of my life later on but right now she was giving me what I needed her to give me. So after the club that night I decided to go to my diner to eat and brought Top Flight with me. We had a ball that night we talked about everything and nothing and we ate and just enjoyed each other's company and I could tell that this was going to blossom into something beautiful. At this point in my life I have basically given up on men and jumped head first into this Lesbian lifestyle once again let me put this disclaimer out I love all my family in the LBGTQ community but I knew that this route that I was taking was leading me further away from my purpose and further into my brokenness. So Top Flight and I went back to my house that night, she was a bit tipsy and too tired to drive all the way to Philly so she stayed with me. We laid in bed and we talked and she kissed me for the first time that night and I was just smitten and had the biggest crush on her so this was nice. After this encounter we would spend a lot of nights just talking on the phone for hours or until she fell asleep which is usually what ended up happening. She was definitely burning the candle at both ends in her life as I was but we were hustlers and that is just what we did and financial security was always the motivation. So we talked for a few weeks and then I found out she had another situation and that she was all over the place so she didn't have any real time for me so I had to leave this where it was before I got any deeper involved. I really liked her as a person because she was just amazing, she was smart, beautiful and just such a hard worker so I wanted to keep her in my life. So fast forward September of 2008 I decided to start a profile on a Lesbian dating site Chile I really was trying to wave my rainbow flag proudly and I was not looking back men at this point were a distant memory. I am such an extremist that I can not do anything half heartedly. I have to go all the way in so here I was jumped right on over to the other team in the middle of the game. Here I am in the middle of all of this brokenness thinking that changing teams will heal my heart and stop me from feeling or thinking about Mr Married Man. Now I will admit it was definitely a bandage for this wounded heart it kept me busy because there is a lot of drama that surrounds this lifestyle and when you start dealing with a bunch of women no matter how manly they may act or look they are still women and they act like it and that was just annoying my life. I was hanging in there though no one was going to knock me off my Pride Flag! I was waving it proudly. At this point I haven't seen or talked to my kids in a few weeks my mother had blocked my number and tried to act like they didn't want to be bothered with me and I knew that was not true but at this point there wasn't much I could do, I didn't have a car and I was working nights so I just tried to deal with it the best I could. My baby girl was 2 already and she was missing and needing her mommy, my son was 8 and he was having behavior issues and he needed me too and my oldest was 12 and he honestly needed me the most and I just couldn't see it because I was so broken and hurt. I kept making one bad decision after the next and it was costing me greatly, not only my things but it was costing me precious time that I could not get back. I had fallen so far that I didn't even think God was even listening to me anymore. I was afraid to even pray because I wasn't ready to stop doing the stuff I was doing.

What I should have been doing was what 1 Peter 5:7 says casting all your care on Him, for He cares for you. I was so focused on running away from this pain and refocusing on other people that I could not see God just wanted me to just give Him my heart so he could heal it properly and take me on my journey to wholeness. So I would ultimately spend my 30s in relationships that didn't serve me or even take care of my true needs, to be truly loved, cherished, respected and cared for. So I met this girl online in September of 2008 for privacy sake she will be called the Tornado because she showed up and just destroyed everything in her path. The level of toxicity and brokenness in this woman's life only highlighted my need to nurture and try and fix this person because I saw from the very first date she needed someone in her life that cared. So I swooped in like the Superwoman I thought I was and it will begin this spiral of madness that became my life for the next 7 and a half years.

Chapter 14

Stormy Weather

Well Tornado and I went on our first date at one of my favorite Jamaican restaurants in Delaware D & H. All my people were there that night just in case she was wack and I could have an exit plan. We had already planned the whole night as a just in case. When she showed up she was cute, she was dressed in this oversized shirt and she was a lot shorter than me, but I enjoyed talking to her, but I should have noticed the amount of alcohol she consumed that night and I seemed to overlook it because the dinner was definitely on her. So I humored her and for the most part I enjoyed myself. We had a decent conversation and then my friend that was with me we will call her highschool friend seemed to know her and was talking about how nice she was and how she was a good person. So I decided to give her a chance. At this point I was not looking for love, I was just looking for security because being in love has just ruined my life, or so I told myself. I couldn't do that again. I wasn't even thinking about anything but becoming stable again, I felt like if I could help her she would help me. This relationship would be functional and beneficial for both parties. So that night we decided to get a hotel because neither one of us could really go back to where we lived at the time. I was renting a room and she was staying with her dad, neither were ideal situations. We spent that night at a hotel on Route 202 and her drinking was definitely excessive because after the 5 drinks she had at the dinner she had a 6 pack of Mike's Hard Cranberry in the car, so then I understood why when we checked her blood sugar at the hotel it just read High. She should have been at the hospital but instead she pulls out this pill that was full of lint and pops it to lower her blood sugar, but not before washing it down with one of those

Alcoholic beverages. Now this is when I would have inserted an eye roll emoji because this was just down right foolish and I was complicit in this health crime. So now my shero complex was in full activation, I was determined to save this woman from herself. In the meantime I was dying on the inside and drowning in my own heartbreak and brokenness but I saw a job that needed to be done so I stepped in. I didn't realize at the time that I was in way over my head. Alcohol wasn't the only battle we were going to be fighting. I will find out early in our relationship she struggled with drugs as well and this will pose to be a bigger issue than I could have even predicted. The first week we were together I took her to my nephews going away party to introduce her to the family and this was a big mistake. She showed out so badly and got so drunk she was in everyone's face, dancing with old ladies and stumbling and falling all over the place and ultimately I would be dragging her drunk behind right on out of there. She was so drunk she fell and scraped her knees all up as I dragged her to the car. I was trying to process how someone that just met my family could behave in this way, but I had to remember what and who I was dealing with she had a major problem and didn't care much about herself or her health and this would be a clear indication she didn't really care about me so embarrassing me didn't phase her one bit. Now let me stop here and say this having a drug or alcohol problem is not a laughing matter and I made light of this situation as a means to bring humor into the story but if anyone you love is dealing with a similar situation they need professional care. All I became in this situation was an enabler because I made excuses for her and I cleaned up every mess her alcohol and drugs ever made and it ultimately consumed my life. That is why I looked up and 7 ½ years had passed and I couldn't tell you where this time went or what I was trying to accomplish with this woman. I looked at her and saw a project and I felt that If I could just help her, maybe I could save her life. I felt though in this moment while I was saving her life I was losing mine very subtly and slowly it creeped up on me before I knew it. So the next incident that would introduce her accompanying drug addiction was this particular evening that she left me at work. I was working at the overnight diner still and I usually got off at 4am and she knew that usually she would come early if she wasnt working and she would order food and sit and talk to me. This particular night I called her and she wouldn't answer and then basically the phone just started going to voicemail. I realized that you can not save anyone that doesn't think anything is wrong with them I knew that her drug issues and her inner chaos had nothing to do with me and my children and everything to do with who she was as a person and I was all done I met this woman in 2008 and I would be in this relationship until 2015 and I would never look back so much has happened during this time My children were mistreated and she felt that because she worked she didn't have to do anything else and she couldn't be more wrong so I will not spend a lot of time in this chapter because this was clearly the longest part of my life My son graduated from High school My other son was going through mental health crisis from the time he was 9yrs old until he was 14yr and this woman's presence just made all of that much worst I can not give her the satisfaction into thinking that she wasn't the worst relationship i had ever been in I was so miserable that I had gained almost 100 pounds and I had surgery after surgery from 2013-2018 my health was suffering even after this relationship was over. The residual effects of it was no joke the stress that weight gain. The depression the food that wasn't good for me and the sleep apnea I was a mess and no one seemed to see the misery I lived under and In 2015 June when I officially let this woman go I had had enough I didn't want anything else to do with her and I was ready to move one with my life. But she couldnt let me go even though she didn't really want me she just thought she owned me chile I don't even know what I was thinking so I move out of that house we had together in November of 2015 and I started my life and she wouldn't leave me alone she thought because she gave me a few dollars that it entitled her to just be in my peaceful place. I like a dummy allowed it. So she lived with me for 6 months and then that was it I made her leave because she wouldn't stop doing drugs and she was always fighting with me. I had been nice long enough. She left and went somewhere and that was that My house was peaceful again.

She was still trying to harass me and I let her know we are all done. Now trust me I had created a soul tie with this woman too. We have spent a lot of time together and even had the nerve to do a commitment ceremony on our 6th year anniversary. I was in deep but the resurfacing of Mr Married man would change the trajectory of my life and this relationship. Now to clear it up she says I left her for this man but ultimately I left her because I was miserable and I deserved so much more than I was receiving from this woman. I needed real true love, I needed to finally walk in the purpose that God had for me and not look back. But as you know I was once again jumping from the frying pan into the fire because this man really didn't change he just got older. So my Married Boyfriend Showed back up as I told you he would now. I haven't seen or spoke to this man since 2008 and in April of 2015 I got this cryptic message on Facebook that says I'm sorry. Now I had no idea who this was or what they were sorry for so I just kept pressing this person to see who they were and what they were talking about. So he finally identified himself and I said to him it was about time. Now I would be lying if I said I didn't think about him from time to time. If I didn't wonder where he was or what he was doing. Now this soul tie never broke and this heart issue was never truly healed. I just kept rolling into relationship after relationship hoping it would ease the pain but it never did. I just dragged people into my life and my brokenness in hopes to ease the pain that I was feeling but it never worked. All it did was create more chaos where God was longing to give me peace and true joy. Even when this man showed back up in my life I had an opportunity to be alone and let God work fully in my life and I still chose to be with this man. So this was the beginning of my new life the chapter where Tornado is out and my man has showed up even though she swore up and down I left her for him but we didn't even officially get together until she was out of my house and he was completely out of his house i don't need to explain myself to any one. Me and this woman broke up in June of 2015 and me and this man didn't officially get together until November 2016 but in her delusion she will think what she wants because she can't handle the fact that I left her and never looked back.

Chapter 15

The New Beginning

Remember I told y'all this Married Man would show up again well after 8 yrs he would come back and we would be in a real relationship oh but trust me it wasn't all peachy keen this dude had some shit with him and I was still trying to figure out how we spent the next 3 yrs together going to concerts and family vacations but honestly he was doing some shit he shouldn't have not been he was lying but I was so in love I didn't see it but my best friend seen it and we would talk all the time and he didn't like her only because he was jealous of her and our friendship only bc she was my best friend and we would do our girls trips I felt like I had to sneak to hang out with my best friend, but i'm getting ahead of myself so to go back this man thought that I was going to allow him to be with me whenever he wanted too and still live with his wife and I let him know in no uncertain terms that that was not going to happen and I was all done he was either going to be with me or stay at his house but he wasn't about to do both. So in November of 2016 this man comes to live with me and at this point I was ecstatic I felt like everything I ever wanted was finally happening for me. This was going to be a cake walk though because I didn't trust him, I was still extremely scarred from all the years prior in this other relationship and all of the things that he had once put me through. He definitely had to sit through a lot of hard conversations with me. We had a lot of long talks unpacking all the things I was feeling over the years, my misconceptions, my insecurities and how I just blamed him for every foul decision I made over the years began and ended with him. Now let me puse for a second and talk about accountability, although this heart issue I had since 2003 was nagging me and altering my ability to make rational decisions I still could have took on the responsibility to govern myself accordingly. I freely made those decisions so I don't blame anyone now I take full account of everything that I have done and every decision that I made in my life following that affair. At this point though I was a little resentful of all that I went through because this man never chose me. I still had so many questions and so many things I needed to say to him so that he would understand the impact he had on my life over the years. We began this relationship and in the beginning it was amazing having my best friend back in my life was surreal and then having this man in my life, in my bed and in my home on a full time basis was definitely a good feeling. This heart issue I had never really healed I just welcomed the man into my life that broke my heart the worst to try and bring all the weight of the last 13 years into this life of ours and try to fix what he broke because I felt at the time that only he could fix it beccause he is the one that broke me.My whole approah to this relationship was already wrong the only one that could completely fix me was Jesus no man could ever have that much power to make me or break me but my mindset still wasnt clear and honestly I was blinded by the sex and the falsities of the love he claimed to have for me. I would be lying if I said I wasn't enjoying this relationship we were going to concerts, we took our first family vacation and my family was overall very happy with how this was going my kids liked this man and my daughter especially liked him and she looked at him as her dad and he treated her like she was his daughter and this made my baby girl so proud. One thing I will say about him is that he was a great father figure to my children and even though my boys were damn near grown it was nice for them to see me in a healthy and happy relationship for a change. Now although I was content and we had definitely got ourselves into a great family routine I was still pretty uneasy about how much time he was spending back at his wife's house and we would have several arguments about that even though he said he was visiting his son I still didn't fully believe him, something in my spirit just couldn't fully believe that he would truly let go of that life he left behind so abruptly and his credibility with me was less than perfect so I still had major questions. I also had an issue that he wouldn't let me tag him in any pictures on facebook and he also had an issue with me putting pictures of me and him on my Social Media and that didn't sit well with me because if we are together than their shouldn't be a problem but he seen it a different way. He felt as though posting pictures of us and tagging him was rubbing it in his family's face and he didn't want to be disrespectful, this is where I would insert the eye roll emoji because I love all the respect he now has but didn't care about having an affair or lying and cheating but pictures are the real problem, alright sir I could see already where this was going and I wasn't comfortable. So time was passing and we were still doing a lot of things together spending our time together and sharing laughs and making memories.SO during this time I was still having health problems and a lot of it was contributing to my weight gain. I had to get Hernia surgery in Dec of 2016 then in July of 2017 I had to get both my Appendix and my Ovary removed because all of my cysts came back and there was nothing that the Dr could do to save it. So now I was going to be thrust into surgical menopause at 39 I didn't understand what was happening or what God was doing I was devastated I still wanted to have at least 1 more child so that I could truly experience what it would feel like to be married and be with someone I loved and have them go through the whole pregnancy with me and do all the cute stuff that it entails. That ship has sailed and as of right now I would never know what that would feel like, each child I had no one was ever there and I was always alone and now the one thing that I always wanted I was not going to be able to have and this broke my heart and made me super sad. So I had to deal with these feelings I was having so much has happened in this year already and I really needed to start seeing someone so that my mental health wouldn't get out of control. So in September of 2017 I started seeing a therapist and it was literally the best thing that I could have ever done for myself. Now this man was supposed to be coming with me as well to unpack some of our relationship issues but he attended 1 session and that was it the next year and a half that I would be in therapy it would be for me, my strength , my elevation the betterment of my and all that I needed for my life. I really started seeing not only myself different from my time in therapy but I started to look at this relationship in a different light and the reasons why I thought I was in love with him were no longer the reasons why I wanted to be with this man. He was in love with the 25 year old me that was broken, confused and didn't know any better and now I was an almost 40 year old woman that looked different and wanted more from life and was going to get it at all costs. So in June of 2018 I had my last and final surgery after a series of unsuccessful medication treatments for this heart condition that I had my cardiologist and my electrophysiologist decided to perform a cardiac ablation so that I would no long have these episodes of Supraventricular Tachycardia or SVT for short. So for those that don't know what that is let me explain: A Faster than normal heart rate beginning above the heart's two lower chambers. SVT Is a rapid heart beat that develops when the normal electrical impulses of the heart are disrupted. I didn't even know I had this until 2016 when I had my first episode while working and had to be rushed to the hospital and my heart rate was 194 and they had to give me medicine in the ambulance before even getting to the hospital. This was pretty scary and I didn't understand it but after this hospitalization I would be getting treated for this, they put me on a cardiac diet for two weeks and I was basically drinking water and eating air because I could not eat a damn thing that was tasty. So after the two weeks I went back to see my doctor and they put me on blood pressure medicine and this would pose to be quite an issue for me because I didn't have any blood pressure issues and this would make me extremely tired and my blood pressure would be very low like 96/55 low like I could have passed out at any time low. So after being on these meds for almost a year I had a very severe attack my heart rate was hovering around the 200 mark for almost an hour and a half and they couldn't find a vein for a line to give me the meds so I was now in the ER with Jump pads on me because they thought I was going to go into cardiac arrest. So the Dr comes in and once they finally got an IV line in he says you are going to feel a sense of doom but it will only last a few seconds so I just start praying and let the peace of God wash over me because they stopped my heart and restarted it while I was awake and I was now in the hospital overnight again and this time I was leaking troponin which is fluid around your heart and they wanted to make sure I didn't have a heart attack. So I am a bit scared but I had to just keep the faith and know that God didn't bring me this far in my life for it to end here so I definitely wanted to live more, I wanted to enjoy my life to the fullest no more stress no more headaches and no more people or things in my life that were no longer serving me and my best interests it was time for a real long lasting change in my life and God was definitely ushering me into the next season of my life with a clear strategy. In the early part of June I decided to get the cardiac ablation procedure done. I had to stay in the hospital overnight and I was not supposed to drive or do anything strenuous for the next 2 weeks. Well of course I couldn't follow those instructions because I had bills due and this Married Man could not help me so the day after I got out the hospital I was Ubering down at the beach because my car note was due and I couldn't rely on him to help. I was doing a whole lot of thinking because I was really tired of working so hard with this man living with me and not being able to do anything but give me penis and concert tickets. It was getting old fast something had to change because if I was going to work this hard I could have stayed alone. So slowly I was pulling away from him and doing my own thing, on June 28th 2018 I got free tickets to the Power Premiere in New York I was so excited because this was my favorite show on TV we watched this show together and it was our show but when I asked him to go with me he said he couldn't his son had a game so I said no problem I will find someone to go with me or I will go myself but I was going. So me and my homegirl started our trip to New York. It was such a fun day everything went smoothly and as we had planned. We met so many amazing people that day I got to meet the whole cast and we took pictures with a lot of them. I was literally living my very best life and I was not apologizing for it. On the way out of Radio City Music Hall I saw this guy and I would be lying to you if I said this brother wasn't fine as I don't know what, So I turn around and say you look like you belong on this cast and he laughed and said thank you. Then we proceeded to talk and joke and we took pictures and I exchanged numbers with this man and this would prove to be a turning point in my life and I didn't even know it. I was already getting tired of all the excuses this man was giving me and I was tired of our lives as it was I was always working and so was he we very rarely spent time together anymore and when he wasn't working he was with his son so we were at a crossroads and I could feel the disconnect so it was not long that I started entertaining conversation from this handsome young man that I had met and he made me feel so good about myself and this was just the jump start that I needed for my beginning exit out of this relationship and on to just loving me and wanting the life that God has for me and not the one that I keep picking for myself. So as I started to elevate in my career and started to look toward my future I decided to start my business, now I had been working for Uber and Lyft since 2016 and I had made them plenty of money all the hours I put in and I would always hear people ask me if they could get me again to be their driver because they just loved me and my personality and wanted me to be their driver but I told them that with these platforms that isn't a possibility but I started to think that I could start a business of my own, I could be the company that fills the gaps that Uber and Lyft leave behind so in November of 2018 We Care Rideshare Inc was born I wanted to be the answer to the problem I wanted to cater to the more vulnerable populations like woman, The elderly and teenagers so that they could get where they needed to go safely and feel confident in the ability of the driver that they chose. So as I drove for Uber and Lyft I was still building my business and on November 17 I had my launch party and all my friends and family showed up for me and it was beautiful and I was so proud of what I was accomplishing I was now a business owner and I planned on being the first transportation company owned by a woman of color to be able to make a dent in this industry. I didn't want to compete with Uber and Lyft. I wanted to do what they didn't so that it was no competition at all because I was creating my own lane. I literally started this business with a dollar and a dream I didn't know how I was going to do it but God said step out on faith and start the business and that is exactly what I did. Now even though all my friends and family came to my party the one person that I expected to be there wasn't and of course he had an excuse for not being there because of drill but he had skipped drill for a lot less before but I didn't argue I just seen where I needed to place him because his level of support was less that Ideal since he was my man I expected a lot more from him and he was disappointing me at every turn. What I would come to realize in my time in therapy was that this man wasn't interested in my elevation or forward movement. He wanted to keep me just like I was so I would be able to keep taking his nonsense without protest and calling it being supportive. Well I was all done supporting someone that couldn't even see my change and growth and celebrate that I needed to be with someone that would celebrate my evolution not resent it. So in December I paid for an office space so that I could conduct interviews and have a business address. I was really taking this business seriously because this would now become my livelihood and it was doing well. I had about 10 clients on my book and that was increasing daily by word of mouth and my business page on FB people were really responding and it was a beautiful thing. God's favor was truly in my life and even in the midst of this sinful relationship God was still blessing me and showing me all that I deserve as a child of the King. So I decide to take a break and go out to Cali to visit a friend and also I had tickets to go to the REAL one of my favorite talk shows on TV I was super excited and of course He didn't think I should go , he was feeling some type of way because I had to leave I wanted to network I was going to talk with some investors and make some deeper connections and I was just going to enjoy myself because I needed this vacation away from everyone so that I could get my whole entire life. So I bought my ticket and on Dec 9 I was out I headed to the airport and my first stop was Denver Colorado to see my best friend and her beautiful new baby. Denver was beautiful. I had never been so this was a new experience for me and I was enjoying every second of it. Then I leave Denver and I head to LA and that was even better the weather was gorgeous and I was definitely taking advantage of all the blessings that God was giving me and although I was away from this man for almost a week I barely missed him, I knew the tides were turning but I just wouldn't know how soon this would all happen and what God had up his sleeve for me in the next upcoming months. So once I get back from

LA I was exhausted because the people I had put in charge of the pickups while I was gone were not doing what they were supposed to do and this will be my first lesson in not trusting anyone with your baby but yourself because no one is going to take care of what's yours better than you. Now as soon as I come back from LA I come home and my son comes running into the room to tell me that my car is gone and i'm like what!? So I start calling all over to see what happen and of course that bank came and repoed my car because I was a month behind and once again I was busting my ass working damn near around the clock and I couldn't pay for everything on my own and this man was not helping me and I was over it. Meanwhile every extra cent he has was going into his wife's household and not mine so on New Years eve I decide to rent a car, and Ironically he was able to help me do that he got a loan and gave me the money to rent this car because I needed to make some money and I needed a car to do it so I start Ubering and doing Lyft again and i'm trying to make as much money as I can to play catch up i'm now starting to think my trip to LA wasn't such a good idea because I was missing so much money. I didn't know it then but this was all part of the plan that God was setting up for me so strategically, He was truly ordering all of my steps even if I don't know yet or even understand my whole life is about to change in a major way. Now things are happening in the spirit realm I don't even see but I was getting closer to God and I was ready to live my life according to the word of God and I wanted God's best for my life and as I was seeing very clearly this man was not it.

Chapter 16

The end of an Era

This relationship of mine was going nowhere fast and little did I know I was about to collide with destiny and it would start my journey into self discovery and healing. On Jan 7 2019 I sent my middle son to Job Corp. It was a push and pull at first but I was able to get him to go and I was so proud of him for making the hard decision of leaving behind everything he knew and doing something positive for his life. He was going to be in Potomac right outside of Washington DC and I believed this would be a great thing for him. He needed this change and this new start. Now I love my children with everything in me and I want nothing but the best for them and this child has been my hardest case, it has been a struggle with this boy from the beginning but he was my special one and I knew God has an amazing plan for his life and I just want to see him stay safe and walk in that. So my baby called me and said he needed some snacks and his wallet that he left at home and me being the mother I am, I have to make sure my child doesn't want for anything if it's in my power to do so. On Sunday Jan 20th 2019 I made the wonderful drive to the Job Corp in DC to take my son what he needed. Now as I'm flipping through Instagram earlier in the weekend I noticed that there was an amazing Martin Luther King day event going on that same day and it looked like it was going to be amazing so I was like i'm going to go to this since I will already be in the area. Little did I know that this event would only be 20 mins from my son's school so this couldn't be more perfect. That day I had asked every one in my house including Mr Married man if they wanted to come and everyone declined so I was like no problem I love to drive and I sure don't mind going alone. So I went out early in the day and did some Uber and Lyft to make some extra money so that I could have all that I needed for this drive. God was with me all day long because I literally made a little over what I needed and so I was on my way. The traffic was light so this was smooth sailing even when I got on the 195 going toward DC it wasn't crowded. I was surprised this day couldn't be more perfect. I could really feel the presence of God all over me and this trip I was taking it was amazing. So I get to my son's school at about 3:30 and give him all his stuff and spend some time talking to him meeting his friends and seeing the campus. It was cold as a hookers heart out that day and it was windy as hell but this was January for you on the East Coast nothing new. So once I look up the address to this event I start heading that way the event started at 5pm and so I was right on time. I found this school without a problem and even got a pretty good parking spot, like Come on Jesus with all these beautiful blessings! It's the little things chile because it was colder than a freezer at the meat market outside and I was cute but I wasn't warm and this jacket I was wearing I couldn't zipper up, This belly chile was in the way I definitely needed to work on this weightloss thing ASAP I thought to myself. So I get into the event and I'm fine with just slinking into the back and minding my business, but nope little Ms Usher has to walk me right to the front row. I was like really? I felt like I had a spotlight on me and I had this bright red jumpsuit on with sparkles on it and I felt like I was glowing under this light and I didn't know why. All of this will make sense soon. I'm sitting there waiting for the event to start and I just feel the peace of God come over me. It was so overwhelming but it was amazing and a little unfamiliar in this setting because I didn't understand at the time what was going on. Out walks the narrator of the evening and he looked so handsome and I just realized we were wearing the same colors. I started to giggle a bit in my spirit because I heard the Spirit of the Lord say there he is and i'm like yes ok and? I see him! So as I'm watching this man do his thing I felt like I was there supporting my husband it was such a strange feeling. So I hear God speak into my spirit again, that is the man I have for you. I was literally arguing with myself in my head because im like why am I hearing this? I didn't ask for this, I'm not looking for this. I have a whole boyfriend that I am living with at home. This isn't making sense but I just keep watching this event and I felt us make eye contact while he was on stage and I could feel this big smile come across my lips and I felt such an warm sense of peace in my spirit and I had this overwhelming sense of familiarity with this man like I have known him my whole life even though I only met him that day. So the event is over and I hear Mr Narrator was doing meet and greets and pictures in the Lobby so I said let me get on out there and say hey. So I waited in line and I talked to the person that I was sitting next to because we have become fast friends and she was a sweet lady. Then it's my turn to go up and take my picture and I had a million butterflies in my stomach it was crazy and this beautiful man looks me in my face and says to me " Hey Beautiful" I could feel my knees weaken and I said to him hey we have the same colors on, and he says " They are good colors now come here girl let's take this picture" I am speechless at this point and all I can say to him is how beautiful he is! Chile this is where I would put the hand over my face emoji because what was I saying and why was I saying that? But shit he was beautiful I wasn't telling no lies. The moment he put his arm around me to take this picture I heard God say again this is the man I have created for you this will be your husband and I wanted to pass out but I had to stay strong and act like I didn't hear what I just heard. So he looked over at me and said " She took at least 6 pictures so your good" I started to giggle and then I took the picture for my new friend since her phone had died and he gave me this beautiful smile and I just blushed and those butterflies were back again. I didn't know what just happened or what I just heard but I was going to need a serious explanation as I drove back home because this didn't make any sense to me, I have never in my life heard God tell me anyone was my husband. I damn sure didn't want to be that weirdo going around saying God told me this man was my husband looking crazy because I'm sure a million women may think the same thing, this man is single, extremely handsome, loves the Lord and is just an amazing person who wouldn't want him to be theirs. I definitely would never have picked someone like him to be my person, I don't want to be with no celebrity or anyone in the limelight and I sure didn't deal with dudes this damn fine he will be a whole problem. I knew this had to be God because I was not one of those women that chases after celebrities or thinks people are their husband so what was going on here Jesus you have some major explaining to do sir. On my drive back home I first had to call my spiritual mom and tell her what I just experienced because I was trying to make sense of it all and I needed some reassurance. So after I get off the phone with my Spiritual mom I just drive in silence I am excited, overwhelmed and a bit confused. I said to the Lord how this is going to work. I live in Delaware and I'm still in a relationship and this man lives 3000 miles away on the other side of the country. Let me take this time to say God's ways are not our ways and his thoughts are not ours so the things that He does and the way He does them wouldn't make a bit of sense in our human mind, as we start to try to make this logical or rational the less sense in makes according to us. As I drove home in silence I heard God say, you heard me correctly now I want you to learn everything about this man and I will show you little by little why I chose him for you and why I chose you for him. Now Mr Married man is still at the house and at this point i'm looking at him like who are you again and why are you here? It was almost like God said let me take care of all of this. I am going to strategically start moving the pieces to this puzzle around and getting rid of things that don't fit. So 2 days later on my birthday Jan 22 2019 this beautiful man and I will have our very first interaction on Instagram and I was just ecstatic what an amazing birthday present! Mr. Married man bought me a cake and didn't even have the decency to even come sing to me. My kids sang to me and we had some cake and little did I know then this man would leave me for good the very next day. He came home that day talking about someone broke into his wife's house while they were at the game and his son was really upset and scared and that he was going to stay over there for a few days and I just looked at him like he had 5 heads and said do whatever you have too i'm good, and I meant every word of that. After work he would go over there and never come back. I got this letter stating that we had until the end of the month to get out of this Apartment because this dude went to the office and gave them fake military papers so that he could get out of that lease. I was like really my dude this is what we are going to do? Ok well now I was completely relying on the Lord and Him ordering my steps in everything I do because my children and I were about to be homeless. I had my 4 kids and my dog during this time I had picked up one of my adopted sons and took him in because he needed me and I was not going to turn my back on him. God immediately started working on my behalf, I was approved for an early refund anticipation loan for 900.00 so I was able to get a Uhaul, Pay movers and get a storage unit for all my stuff and pay for an AirBNB for a week so my children and I were not in the street. God would start to show himself strong in my life because at this point I was saying yes to Him and no to everything else and I have finally given the Lord this heart to heal completely so I could be whole and complete in my life lacking nothing. I was determined this time not to make any of the crazy mistakes I made before because of this heart issue. If I said I wasn't sad I would not be telling the truth and there were a few nights that I cried myself to sleep once my life calmed down and I really processed what had truly happened this was most definitely an end of an era and this will complete the reign of terror and heartbreak this man had on me for the last 17 years I was giving all this over to God because I knew now what and who He had for me and I wasn't going to forfeit my blessings looking behind me. God allowed me to be with this man for this length of time so that I could see him for the broken and troubled man that he was and at this point all I could do is pray for him but I was going to move on with my life and I was going to leave this life behind me once and for all. Can I say this will be easy? Absolutely not I was going to deal with some of the hardest times of my life, but I knew as long as I had the Lord by my side there wasn't anything that I couldn't endure. What was so amazing is that every day I went to this beautiful man's page and there was something that he would say or post that would resonate with my spirit and my situation and it would just pull everything right back into perspective. Even from thousands of miles away I felt so spiritually connected to this man and it was so amazing and so God all the way. God was still blessing me and showing me what my next moves are I took a job working with a child at a Jewish school outside of Philly and it was truly a blessing because im not working for anyone but myself and this job is under my business and im getting paid 500 a week to work with this child and it was a major blessing. In the midst of that I am learning more about the Jewish culture and I'm even learning Hebrew this was definitely a blessing from the Lord. I would start Ubering the moment I was out of that Job so that I could make sure I had enough money to not only pay for this car I was still renting but the Air BNBs that I now had to stay at because I didn't have a place yet. This was all overwhelming but I had to keep myself busy and working so that we wouldn't end up in the street. My kids were definitely hanging in there with me and this was not easy especially with this dog it was super difficult and there were days I would resent this man and get angry with him all over again and I would have to remind myself that this was God's divine plan and it will all work itself out eventually. I started making some amazing friends in the Air bNB Game and there were people that would be a blessing to me giving me a cheaper rate or even an off the books stay God was really taking care of me. I'm so glad that I got that office and I still had it and was paying for that monthly and after I told my office landlords what I was going through they allowed me to stay in the basement for a few days where there was a bed and they had a shower there and even a place that we could make food it was truly a blessing. God was truly making provision for my life and I could see his hand at work,

This wasn't ideal but it was provision nonetheless and I was thankful, I woke up every day with joy in my heart and a song on my lips. God had told me to start making videos for my Instagram to just be inspirational and I did and it was almost like me and the hubby were talking to each other in these videos and he would even like my posts if I tagged him in them it was really awesome and it was him just letting me know subtly that I see you and I appreciate you. At this time in my life I needed that more than anyone would know, that encouragement and reassurance was everything to me. He just didn't know how he was already changing my life for the better. He was really healing me and didn't even know it. So as time went on I had gotten rid of this rental car that was costing me way too much money and bought a car, now I know I was a bit hasty and I should of waited but I needed a car and so I went to the one place that I knew would give me one no questions asked as long as I had the money to put down. This would prove to be a big mistake because this car was a lemon and it was causing me problems already. This is where God is still working on me with impatience and my impulsivity. I am just at the beginning of my journey to wholeness and so my need to fix situations and so things on my own when things are not moving fast enough is one of my biggest problems and God would deal with me swiftly on that. This car wasn't worth the down payment I put on it and all the things that needed to be fixed on it was ridiculous. So I just stopped paying on it and eventually they shut it down and once again not having a car was extremely inconvenient because i had too much to do in my life and not having a car was going to prove to be a big issue for me. In the midst of all of this I needed to take a mini vacation, now I know this isn't the time or even the right scenario to be taking a vacation but I needed this more than I will know I found out my husband is going to be in Vegas in March and I asked God am I supposed to go to this event? If this is what i'm supposed to be doing Lord make it so bring me all the finances I need to make it happen. That is exactly what He did. My son came to me that night and said, " Mom, I have this 300.00 on this card and I can't take any money off of it if I give it to you, can you give me the cash when you get paid"? I said I sure can! Now I had every penny for this event. I couldn't believe it! How swiftly God answered my prayer concerning this man and this trip it was so crazy to me. My kids were not very happy about the fact that I was going to Vegas and we still didn't have a place to live and we were still at these Air BNBS but this trip would prove to be more than a vacation some major things would happen that would change the course of my life and usher me into my real life wilderness experience. On March 27th I rented a car and all the money I needed to do all of this was right where I needed it to be. God was at work again in this situation I was in awe. Every time anything I was doing had to do with this man it was a very peaceful and seamless transition and everything would just fall into place, these confirmations were coming more and more now I have bought both his books, downloaded his music and started watching all his shows and interviews I was really getting to know alot about this man because honestly I didn't know much about him and I was pleasantly surprised by all I was learning about him and it was all tying together nicely with what God was telling me.

Chapter 17

The New Regime

My real and true healing was under way and I was feeling really good about my life, I have pure joy and I am so excited about this trip, I have never been to Vegas and I am going by myself so I drive to the airport in the middle of the night I left Reading after dropping off my daughter with my Stepmom and I started to drive to New Jersey I was flying out of Newark International this was all new for me. I have never flown out of this airport but I made it there by 4;30 in the morning my flight left at 7:00am and I was right on time not rushed, plenty of time to spare and I returned my car and I started my venture to find my Terminal. I have never been more excited to see anyone these butterflies are back at the very thought of seeing his handsome face again. Never knew real and true love that comes from the Lord could feel this amazing, it is the most wholesome and pure feeling I wouldn't trade it for all the money in the world because this makes me feel like i'm not only rich but wealthy, wealthy in the favor of God and that is something money can't buy. So I board my plane finally and I meet folks on the plane and start chatting it up and just having a great time. This trip is about to be a whole blast already I could tell. So I got to Vegas and I booked my room at the Rio because it was cheap and that is where the conference was and so it was a win win for me. I was exhausted from all this flying and driving and I remembered I really didn't have much sleep I slept for a few on that 5 hour flight but my excitement was definitely keeping me awake so when I get to the hotel and settle in I shower and I go right to sleep and woke up and it was about 8 pm and I needed some food, I checked his Instagram and I noticed he was on his way to Vegas he had this crazy Uber story and his trip wasn't as smooth and seamless as mine but in a few hours I will see his handsome face and he will see my beautiful face and all of that will be a distant memory. He was only at the event for one day so I was going to make it a point to make the most out of it, this was my time to really show him who I am and my personality, I brought him a gift because God put it on my heart to be a blessing to him and I wanted to give him something thoughtful. I bought him a notebook that said Think Big on it because his word of 2019 was Bigger so this was perfect and then I got him a jar full of inspirational quotes called 30 days of greatness. I also bought him a card and put a handwritten note in there to tell him how much he has impacted my life and got me through some pretty dark days and of course in true female fashion I put my perfume all over the card so that the moment he would smell it he would think of me. I was going to make sure he knew me and remembered me because like Ruth in the bible I had to present myself to him, I wasn't thirsty but I was shrewd because I knew who I was and I was walking in God's Confidence because I have a word from the Lord backing me up so this makes me very confident in what I am doing. The event starts and i'm sitting there in the audience and just watching everything around me and then all of a sudden I see him sitting at a table and those butterflies start again and im giddy like a schoolgirl, Chile I was nervous and excited all at the same time but it was a feeling I will never forget because I had never felt this way about someone that I barely knew, even though it felt like I knew him my whole life it's so strange. I will soon find out that that feeling of knowing him forever is because this relationship was ordained from the foundation of the world and the instant we met my soul recognized his soul because i have been looking for him my whole life and I now know that he has been looking for me as well it is a literal mind blowing experience and something I am having trouble describing because it is truly a spiritual connection that can only be explained by God arranging this meeting and being all over it. Every Time I was with this man or around this man I felt the presence of God and it was miraculously marvelous. At this point the conference is underway and I'm watching him interact with the fans and it's so fun to watch. I'm texting my friend and sending her pictures because I'm so excited that he is there, I don't know what to do and I don't want to make any mistakes or say anything silly out of nervousness. I'm watching the autograph line and I wait for it to die down and then I make my move I slide on in there and I purchase one of his books and I asked him if he could sign it and he says sure and asked me how to spell my name and then here come the autograph police, this lady asked me 8 different ways if I had an autograph ticket and I told her each time no but I just bought a book and would like for him to sign it. I could not believe they would not let this man sign a book I paid 20$ for and they expected me to purchase a 40$ ticket to get him to sign my book um sorry miss but your trippin and that would be a No for me. So he gives me prayer hands and mouths he is sorry and then says I just work here and I smiled at him and said its ok its not your fault. I wanted to give him his gift then, but I chickened out and that autograph debacle had me heated so I held onto my gift that has now been through so much it was traveling with me all this time and I still managed to keep it intact. It was still early in the day. I will wait until later to give him this gift. I just enjoyed watching him in his element, to see all the fans excited to see him to watch him working and enjoying the interactions. It was such a treat for me, I felt like I was getting a close up of our lives together and it was beautiful and exciting. One thing about me is I have no fear, and I get in where I fit in with the most respectful confidence so the next event was the Q&A Panel and I was a bit late because I ordered tacos and it messed my whole schedule up because I missed out on signing up for the Karaoke. I slide on into the line and I'm the last person to ask him a Question so he spends a minute and 30 seconds answering my question and I was smitten, I had those butterflies back again and I had to stay strong and ask my question with assurance. At this point I am well versed in who he is and I have done a lot of research. I have read both books, I have listened to every song he has on Spotify and I have watched a lot of his interviews so I am armed and ready so I can ask an educated question. I felt good and confident and after he answered my question and I looked back at the video later on I noticed him spend a few seconds watching me walk away and in my mind watching that showed me that he was equally as smitten, he was just going to be a bit more cautious. Now it's time for this photo and I have waited all day for this because it's not just a picture with my phone they are taking a professional picture of us and I was just excited to be in his presence again because he makes me giddy like a schoolgirl. My plan was to be the last in line again so that I could spend some time just talking to him because I just love his spirit and he is so funny. So it's my turn and he was like well hello again, I was like in my mind he remembered me! Those butterflies are back in full force, I felt like he could hear them fluttering in there. They were so busy, my heart was literally beating out of my chest and I was hoping he couldn't see that because I did have the girls out! I ask him how we are taking this picture, he says' ' However you want it's your picture" I was like well you don't have to tell me twice. I suggested the prom pose, which would have this man's arms around me while he stood behind me Chile It got real hot all of a sudden because being this close to him had these knees weak again. Of course i'm just cutting up as usual because I just say anything,I was like wait let me fix the girls and he turned his head and said "Go head fix the girls" At this point im cracking up and so was he it was such a beautiful moment he put his arms around me and I intertwined my fingers in his and I felt this heat and electricity flow through me and I was like whoa. I was wondering if he felt the same because it was so powerful I felt the presence of God all over this. I have all this happening who would even believe me if I tell them, I had so many things swirling around in my head. This was just another indication that what God spoke into my spirit was real and true and I just had to walk this out and get myself together. I still had one more event to attend with him in it and I was looking forward to seeing his handsome face one more time I was hoping that I would get to talk to him and exchange numbers but that was not in the plan just yet but what happened was definitely solidifying my word from God and I will just let God lead no matter how excited I am to be around this man. We are at the last event of the evening and it's Karaoke and as he stood on stage as see him scanning the crowd as if he was looking for me, it was super romantic. This connection was serious and I know he feels it too. Each song he would make sure he made his way down to the area I was standing, and I would just smile and sing my heart out. I was having such a good time I didn't want this night to end. I watched on stage singing and I couldn't help but think, he has been here all day. Is he tired? Has he had enough to eat? Is he thirsty? I went from fan to wife mode and as people were screaming for more of him I was concerned for his well being.

The night was over and I was praying that he would open his gift and see that I put my number in that card and call me so we could just have a conversation. God's timing is perfect. I can not rush what God is doing and I don't want anything out of its season because I still wasn't ready and there was this little pesky thing in between us at the moment called 3000 miles but soon God would change that too. This trip would become more than just a vacation. I would meet people that would change my life forever and set my life on a course to collide me with destiny and all God had for me. While I'm here I met someone that was interested in subletting his apartment and at this point things weren't exactly going well back in Delaware. I had no car, no concrete place to live and the doors that I thought were going to open never did and I felt in my spirit it was time to leave Delaware but I just didn't know where I was supposed to go next. Was I going to be moving to Las Vegas? Is this the place you have in your plan for me Lord? I prayed on it that night, and then I called my Spiritual mother and she confirmed what God had spoke into my spirit and so it was official I was moving to Vegas and this will prove to be a faith walk from beginning to end with no room for me to lean on my own understanding because it just won't make any sense to a carnal mind. I flew back East on April 3 and now I put my plan in motion to get moving and head on out West, I didn't share this with many people because I didn't have time for people to try and talk me out of doing what God said to do. I started getting my affairs in order, God told me I couldnt take anything but what would fit in my rental, so everything that I had in storage was going to have to stay there no matter how much I might want it. So during this time Mr Married man was still lingering around trying to be "helpful" he was trying to rent me a car so that I could start my drive but things just were not working out the way I thought they would, It was because this man was involved and of course because I didn't have my car he was picking me up and taking me places trying to pull that I miss you nonsense, at this point I was feeling like everything that he was doing for me was owed to me for leaving me and my family displaced. There was just something not right about these encounters though and at least twice during this time he almost got into car accidents and I was not about to let this brotha kill me and my family so I texted my spiritual mom and told her to pray because his driving was scaring me. God had his hand on my life and no weapon that the enemy was trying to form against me was going to prosper so I just had to stand strong, keep my armor applied and walk in my anointing.

I wanted to stop here and share with y'all a letter that I wrote to my husband when I got back from Vacation the letter is dated April 10, 2019 11:23pm

Dear Husband,

I thought you would never find me, a string of failed relationships and rejection had me believing the lie that you would never come. But you are here now and I know who you are. I have felt your touch, seen the gleam in your eye when you see me, have felt your arms around me even if it was for just a moment. God allowed me to be in your presence briefly and it was the most amazing time of my life. This connection we share even from miles away is breathtaking, it makes me smile knowing God created you just for me and me just for you. I'm cleaning out my heart, cleaning out my life making room for you. I'm allowing God to heal those broken places so nothing that has happened to me will be evident to you. You will see me healed, whole and ready to receive all the love and affection you have to offer. I will be ready to love you completely just the way you long to be loved the way God intended that Agape love that knows no bounds, no limits. People will see us and smile because we look like two teenagers in love, like we have never known hurt, or pain disappointment or shame. We will enjoy this new feeling that both of us have always wanted but never received. This spiritual connection is so deep even from miles away I can feel your loneliness, joy and every other emotion that you may be feeling throughout the day. This union is predestined and I can not wait to tell you what you mean to me even before we truly become one.

Love your wife

Chapter 18

My Wilderness Experience

On April 15 I started this journey which would be about a week long, Mr Married man showed up and rented me a car for the day and this was perfect I was going to start this journey and see where God would lead. I got the rental it was small and I felt like the dude from the Incredibles in this car all scrunched up but I was going to make it do what it do. That day I drove down to VA to see my Titi and my Cousin and my sister. I couldn't leave without seeing them. It had been way too long and thankfully before I left Reading I was able to see my dad and he was able to see his grandkids so that was definitely a blessing. God is truly closing all these doors and making this transition relatively smooth. I tried to go to storage despite being disobedient because I wanted my jackets and there was a Padlock on my unit so I couldn't get anything. God said what He said and I was still playing. I start my drive toward Virginia and I get there with a decent amount of time to spare and the next day dropped this car off at a rental car place close by, this man was blowing up my phone all frantic telling me I was going to have to come back to Delaware with that car and I said the devil is a lie I will do no such thing. I took that car to a local Avis and let them know that the Check engine light was on and I didn't feel comfortable driving it back to Delaware and they took that care back and no extra charges were going to be incurred. There was no way that car was going to make it all the way to Vegas and God had a different plan anyway. So initially I was going to drive out West with my friend that was going to California but there was just so much Chaos surrounding this God said no this will not be the way I have for you just trust me and follow my instructions and I did exactly that. No matter how people thought I was crazy, or thought that my plan just sounded illogical I know what God said and I wasn't backing down off of that. I'm visiting with the family and having a good time but I knew that time was ticking and God needed me to get moving so I decided I was going to rent a car. I didn't know how I was going to get the money but I knew God would provide. Now as I told yall in the beginning this was a pure faith walk from beginning to end and this was truly my coming out of Egypt story heading into my Wilderness God was providing every step of the way. I felt led to reach out to my new big bro out in Vegas who I met while on vacation, he had become a great friend and support system he would call me to check on me, sent me scriptures and sermons he was really an amazing asset to my life in this season. I called him and told him my dilemma and he said I got you. I will send you what you need to rent the car and start heading out here let's make it happen! I was like look at God and I followed God's instructions on this thing to the letter. I rented the car and I started my trek out West on April 18 2019 these dates would prove to be so significant to me and in the spirit realm. This would be the first time my children had ever been on the West Coast so we are definitely making memories. We are literally driving across the country and God will be with us all the way. I started this drive with 17.00 in my bank account and so I knew God was going to have to make a way because gas alone was going to be triple that. Everytime I swiped my card I was able to fill my whole tank up and only 1.00 came out! I was like wow! Look at God! This is God's provision in action: he was giving me my daily bread. Our first stop along this journey would be to Chicago. I always wanted to go there and my adopted nephew is there and I get to see him hang out and take a little nap before we keep going. Chicago was beautiful, but windy and cold and it was April! I decided to take the kids for some authentic Chicago pizza because why not we are here and this is a once in a lifetime experience and I wanted them to have the full experience. This was definitely a road trip to remember we have a nice SUV and we are cruising. The next stop will be Denver CO and we will get there on National Smoke out day and my son will have himself a ball. I was stopping to see my best friend and her family. I miss her and she is now only a 10 hour drive away or a 2 hr plane ride so this was going to be dope. We will definitely spend the night here because I needed to have a full night's sleep and a shower and we needed clean clothes. So I was so thankful for this break in travel and we were right on schedule. We leave the next morning which is Easter Sunday or Resurrection Day as I like to call it. This was not a coincidence God was definitely in these details. We crossed this threshold in Las Vegas about 9pm and we had made it! We made a few pit stops to buy gas and to see some sights in Utah this was a full experience and I wanted my children to remember this road trip forever because not only did we get to make a cross country trip we were in states we have never even been too let alone seen before and it was a bonding and memorable experience. Now I didn't touch much on this because I wanted to tie it into the story at the right time I was wondering why I wasn't hearing from the Rental car company because at this point the car is a day late and no one has emailed us or called and I thought that was strange but I heard in my spirit there was a glitch in the system. This will not mean anything until I tell the full story now I am truly walking this thing out with blind faith. I am trusting God fully because I don't have any other choice every move I make and every step I take God is directing me. I am staying in prayer and allowing God to speak and I am hearing from him everyday. Once we are in Las Vegas we head to the Apartment to meet with my friend and we pick up our keys and move our stuff in. The place is fully furnished so we don't have to worry about that, I'm thinking to myself God has set us up so nicely this is just how it's supposed to be. Now it's the next day April 22 and I called the rental car company to see how much I owed them because the car was now late, and this lady proceeds to tell me that my rental agreement is not valid because my car was returned. I was like what? Now I did hear God say a glitch in the system and now that was confirmed and it made a lot of sense I was like wow. So I called the corporate office because I didn't want any static. This could get hairy and I want to make sure I make all the right moves. To cover my own self so I called the corporate because I knew those calls were recorded and if need be this could be pulled back up again. God was truly supplying my needs by any means necessary. I also wanted to head to the local rental company as well just to see what the deal is and what I can do, there is no numbers on these keys and they have no record of this car so this local place says just wait for corporate to call you back to tell you what to do because if you leave it here then you will be abandoning the vehicle and still could be responsible for it financially. I said ok then and went on about my business and kept driving and along the course of time having this car still will prove to be an asset to my life because some shady stuff started going down. All of a sudden this so called friend of mine starts to do some really spiteful stuff, now he wanted me to have 700 to give him and I didn't have it but the moment I got there I was on it I went to apply for all my benefits, I was going on job interviews and I had to find a church. I was coming home from the store one day and I was at the light and God said look over that going to be your church and I said ok Lord and I looked up their service times and that was it I started going that Wednesday night for midweek service. Let me just explain really God works in seasons and even if we think people are supposed to be in our lives for a long period of time God will show you quickly if you are listening that this was all temporary and that no matter what I am the source and everyone that comes into your life is just a resource so no one will get puffed up and think because they take something from you it's going to break you. This man that was subletting his apartment to us all of a sudden started flipping the script, after 2 weeks he came and took all the furniture and said his daughter needed it. I just laughed and said whatever you need to do is fine, I was unbothered because I knew God had a plan. Then he took the Key Fob which basically was our way to get into the complex because it was a gated community. My son had to jump the wall everytime we all went out together and I was just like really? Once again I had to remember God is my source and this was just a resource and really he wasn't even that he was just an avenue God used to fulfill his will for my life and this person would be a momentary fixture and would no longer be a part of my life after this. At this point I am working feverishly to get all my ducks in a row because I knew something else was about to happen because this dude couldn't be trusted. I obtained my business license, then I was doing all the necessary things so I could get my Registered Behavior Technician Certification so I can work in the ABA Field here in Nevada. For anyone that doesnt know what ABA is I was working with children with Autism and other Developmental delays and I was conducting behavioral Therapy and modification. I'm not wasting a second. I started looking for places and I was doing all I could to give God something to bless. So about 2 weeks into staying at this man's apartment he comes to me and says I need to get this place out of my name because I'm moving back to New York. I was like ok sir, now i'm getting the hint he wants us out and that's ok God has already prepared me and was telling me what to do and ordering my steps, I had a job lined up and I had a church family that was being a blessing to me already and I knew God was all over this. I went to take my test for my RBT and I passed! I was so excited and one of the ladies from my church paid for all the fees that it would cost me to get this Certification. I was so excited. Once I had this certification I started going on interviews and the first job I was hired at started me off at 18.00 an hour so I knew that this would be a blessing this was definitely my seed that God was blessing me with to move on to the next phase of this season. I had went to see a house a few days before I was supposed to be out of this man's apartment and the place was beautiful and I heard God Speak into my spirit this would be my place, I didn't know for how long but I knew that this was my blessing and I was here for all of it God was just showing off. So I did all the application stuff and on May 23 I had to leave out of this apartment and I didn't know where we were going but I knew God had it and was going to make a way. I was in prayer most of the day listening for God to direct me and I was at the park and the kids were feeding the ducks and I was in the car just praying and meditating and when I was done I jumped on IG and seen my husbands latest post and he was showing this beautiful Villa he was at in the DR and as im laughing and feeling his joy and excitement, I get a call it was the woman about the home I looked at, she said we got the house! I just started to scream and jump up and down I told the kids and they were so excited! This place was fully furnished with everything inside down to the silverware. It was amazing and truly a provision from the Lord I was in Awe. We moved in that Friday which would be Memorial Day weekend. I was finally able to breathe for a minute and allow God to minister to my spirit and show me how well he takes care of His children when they are obedient. So now we are relaxing and enjoying this new place, it had been months since we had our own place and this was such a blessing all I could do was just praise God. SOmething in my spirit just didn't sit well with these people that owned this house they were asking me to send this rent money and security deposit via Zelle and I thought that was strange and I went to this place to pick up the lease and they gave me two copies but neither of them were signed by anyone but me. So the money I had given them I immediately put a stop payment on because none of this is making sense. After speaking to my realtor friend she basically said without all signatures on the lease it was invalid and at anytime they could just put us out, now i'm not going to let that happen and i'm going to get to the bottom of this I go to the court and file a suit and they advised me not to give anyone anything until I have a valid signed lease. What was amazing was that this was June and the court was backed up. They could not even see us Until July 15 so at this point we will have basically been in this house rent free. God's provision is amazing and all I could say is that he was really giving me my daily bread and I was seeing his miraculous provision in action and I was just so blessed. In the midst of all this God is really healing my heart and removing this soul tie that I had with this Married Man. Every now and then a thought would pop up and I would text him and I knew I didn't want to be doing this, I hads to let this man go completely I had something amazing waiting on the other side of this healing and I was not going to let t his familiar spirit keep holding me back and blocking my blessings. I was praying and allowing God to reveal things to me and He had shown me what type of Soul Tie this was and why it has been so difficult to shake this was a fish hook type of soul tie and these are very difficult to break. One night I had a little gathering at my house and the ladies from church came over and anointed the house with me and prayed and ministered to me and during my worship time I seen a vision of that man and in the vision he zippered down his face and a dragon popped out and I knew then this was not an ordinary soul tie, and also she told me that this man would have killed me and my whole family. This was the scariest revelation because I thought back to his erratic driving that almost got us into accidents and my children were with me. I was praising God so much more now because I was completely free and delivered from this man and all that came with him. Even though I was healed and set free there was still this need to stay in contact with him, accept money from him I needed to let this man go completely and never look back, we could not even be friends. I'm just enjoying my blessings and living my best life and this was about to get even more amazing one of my favorite Hip Hop Artists was going to be coming to Vegas and I have been talking about meeting this man for years and he was definitely on my Top 5 list of favorite MCs of all time. I just loved his mind, he was brilliant and his music was everything. So i bought my VIP package which included second row seats, an autographed book, a key chain and a meet and greet and photo with this man. I was all in and I was super excited! I couldn't wait, this would be a once in a lifetime memory and I was going to take full advantage. These are the little nuggets God will bless us with when we are in the right place and being obedient to God's word and walking in his calling.

The excitement I felt to be able to go to this concert was amazing. I had the absolute best time and I couldn't believe I was actually standing in this man's presence and talking to him, I even brought him a gift I was just ecstatic! So I was rocking the whole time and couldn't sit down. This was one of the best concerts I have been to in a while and it was worth every single penny this man is truly an entertainer. Then this brother did a full B- Boy spin on the stage and busted out into a full break dance move. I was in Awe this was super exciting and as the kids would say we were lit! This would definitely be a night to remember for sure and I would cherish this memory for the rest of my life.

I didn't realize then how much this night was going to mean to me because on July 25 Sherrifs would come knocking on my door and tell me that I needed to get out of my house. I was like what is happening right now? Well I would find out this place was a rental scam and I had no legal right to be in that house and we needed to go. I was thankful that this particular sheriff saw the distress on my face and my childrens face and allowed us to gather all of our things and go on our way. As I sat in this car I was trying to figure out my next move and I truly needed God's Guidance because I wasn't expecting this right now. Even though I had a dream a few nights ago that the owners came back and I had to leave so I guess that was a premonition that I should have taken a bit more seriously. Well now we are back without a home and I can not understand what is happening. So many questions swirled around in my head, I had to keep reminding myself that either I'm going to trust God at this moment or not. Either I am going to let the peace of God wash over me and understand that He will make a way out of no way no matter how it looks right now. My kids were distraught, traumatized and not trying to hear me say God got it because there may have been a place deep down that was a little fearful about what was going to happen and how this was all going to work out. I did all the things that I had to do that day, even went to work, put a smile on my face and walked in the confidence that God was watching and He would not leave me nor forsake me. I was doing all the right things, I have been faithful and surely God will open a door for us. That night my children and I slept in the parking lot of the Rio hotel, as I watched my babies sleep and looked in that car and saw everything I owned shoved into the back I was trying to figure out where God was in all of this. What was the lesson Lord I am learning here? What is the testimony that will come out of these circumstances. God was testing me, the same way you praised me when you were living in that fully furnished beautiful 3 bedroom home will have to be the same way you praise me now sleeping in this car in this Casino Parking lot. To add to the stress of this night as we were going into the hotel to use the bathroom we saw about a million grasshoppers flying all around the door and falling on us as we were walking into the door. My baby girl was done if she could have passed out right there she would have because she was beyond afraid and traumatized by these things, that have now descended down on Las Vegas. The morning comes and I wake up and just start to pray and thank God for another day for keeping us safe and allowing us to see another day. I read my devotional and I just start to cry because it is speaking to everything that was happening in my life right at that moment, I call my Spiritual mom and I tell her how good God is and what my devotional says and she prays with me and I feel this overwhelming sense of peace in my spirit and I know that God is on the throne of my life and he is ushering me into my next assignment. I got a call from one of my friends from the church I was attending at the time and she said God had put it on her heart to bring us there for the weekend. I prayed on it and asked God what He wanted me to do while I was there, and give me the wisdom to complete this assignment and all that he has for me to do while I am here. Now let me just pause and say this my whole entire journey when I got to this Wilderness has been a faith walk, I was not making a move without the guidance of the holy spirit and if it didn't sit right with my spirit I didn't do it. This weekend will turn into a few months and it was not easy with two damn near grown children that hated living with people no matter how nice they seemed. I knew this was definitely a warfare situation I was under and God sent me there to wreak havoc on whatever the enemy was trying to do in this household and the people in it. I just wanted to speak life and allow God to use me in a mighty way and watch him move on my behalf. On July 28th my friend and a few other people at the church had paid for me to be a part of The Holy Spirit Conference one of our Local Mega Churches was having, I was so blessed by this event and watched God move and his glory be shown these next 4 days. On the last day of the conference I had received a prophetic word and I was just in awe at God's Goodness and His Grace, these ladies that prophesied to me didn't know me from a can of paint, Told me what my gifts were, and just a few days prior I did a Gifts assessment and the Holy spirit revealed to me one of my gifts was exhortation, and for anyone that doesnt know what that is the definition of that is: an address or communication emphatically urging someone to do something. Now in layman's terms basically it means that I have the gift to encourage people and to assist them in doing what is good for their lives. She also told me that my smile was like a breaker anointing and I never realized that people were always drawn to me and the moment I smile it just draws them to me even more and this was all a gift from God so that I can do what He has called me to do and be able to be effective at it. This was such an eye opening experience because nothing that was said was new to me; it was a reminder or a confirmation of what God had already revealed. I was just in such awe at all that God was doing in my life but one thing she did say is that I have a prophetic gift and that I was going to have to get under someone that would be able to gird me up in that and basically groom me to walk in that prophetic gift. Now that I was armed with this information, I was now looking to be led to that person that God would bring into my life for that specific purpose. This conference had become the biggest blessing for me and during this time God had added another gift for my arsenal and it was healing, The Pastor on one of the nights of the conference had called up to the front anyone that was having a tingling or hot feeling in their hands and I was feeling that! So I went to the front and he prayed over all of us and then had Us turn around and start praying for people! This is completely out of my comfort zone and I wasn't expecting this, but the word of God says to be ready in season and out of season so I went on to pray for everyone that came my way and my hands became hotter and hotter and I was like whoa! I knew this was the beginning of me walking into the ministry God has for me and I was ready no matter what my flesh was trying to tell me. I get home and I want to just heal everything my hands are still hot and I lay them on my son and he was like mom your hands are hot as hell! I just started to laugh and say come on get you some of these hot hands and that became my nickname Hot Hands. I was here for all of it though because I wanted to be all God wanted me to be and I wanted to allow the Holy Spirit to work through me anytime and anyplace. I was now given a new found sense of purpose and I was armed and ready to start being used by God and I was diving head first into the ministry I was even Baptized on June 29 2019 I overcame every fear to be able to do that because I can not swim and I was really afraid of the water because I had almost drowned a few times. This was a true faith act and knowing God was by my side and trusting my Pastor to bring me up out of that water at the right time. I was scared and shaking but I overcame every fear because this was something that I needed to do for this stage of my life, it was symbolic of God cleansing me from my past and sealing this deliverance. I came out of that water feeling cleansed and new and ready for all that God was bringing me and all that would take place in my life from that day forward. I didn't realize it then but this was all a preparation period in my life, God had so many things He needed to get to me and I had to be in the right place to receive all that God was ready to give me and more now was my time and the Joseph anointing was on my life and I had heard that again and I knew that God was about to do a major shift in my life I just didn't know how dramatic it was about to be. See we get all excited when we think about having the anointing of one of these biblical celebrities, especially Joseph we are all like Yes Lord take me from the Pit to the Palace, but we forget all that he endured in the middle of all those prophecies coming to past. That man suffered for no fault of his own. He was sold into slavery by his jealous brothers, falsely accused and imprisoned for 3 years and during that time forgotten by the very people he helped that was supposed to look out. We all want the Palace but we don't want what happens in the middle of that because it is just too much. This is why I named this book in the Middle of it all because I need people to know this middle part isn't glamorous and it's definitely not for the faint of heart this is a battle only the strongest soldiers can endure because if you're not careful this middle can take you all the way out the game. So God was really perfecting my character and testing my strength and boundaries during this time, living with people is never easy and as I said before no matter how nice they are or how well meaning nobody really wants 3 extra people living with them. I tried to stay out of the house as much as possible so that we wouldn't be a bother to anyone. So an opportunity comes up for us to rent rooms out for just 1000 a month, now I was working and making at least 1500 or more a month so this was a good deal My daughter and I would share a room and my son would have his own room and we would have a separate fridge and basically a whole up stairs Loft to ourselves including our own bathroom. I felt this was worth this price and this lady lived alone so I was helping her as she was helping me. I paid her the first 300 upon moving in and I was like ok now I can rest and breathe a little easier. I enrolled my daughter into school and she could walk to and from school because it was literally right across the street. I'm just thanking God because this is such a blessing for me, I just knew that God was all over this and I felt sure that this would be a place I could be for a few months until I figure out my next move. Three weeks after I move in I have my friend come over and do our nails and we are talking and laughing and having a good time. This lady says "Wow Jamie you sure know a lot of people, I have been here a lot longer and don't know as many people as you" I thought this was a strange thing to say and I was trying to figure out what she meant by all of that and I would find out soon enough. A few days later this lady comes to me and tells me that her parents are coming in from Mexico and she needed the room that I was staying in and they stayed for a few months, so basically we were going to have to go. I was trying to understand what was happening, and I was trying not to beat this lady up in her own house because I had moved in, Cleaned out that room and the bathroom and made it hospitable, put my daughter in school all for this lady to tell me to leave! I had to really pray and seek God's face about what was happening and then this woman proceeded to say "Well you know a lot of people you will be fine" I wanted to jump across that bed and strangle her so now her true feelings came out. It's funny that jealousy rears its head in different ways for different people. Sometime it's not what you have that people are always jealous of you it could just be the way other people love you that makes them jealous of you, but at any rate we were back to sleeping on my friends couch and I wasn't happy about it this moving constantly was really starting to take a toll on me and I know the kids were feeling it too even if they don't verbalize it this was weighty.

Maintaining my joy and an attitude of gratitude was not easy but I had to remember that scripture in Phillipians where Paul says: " I know what it is to be in need, and I know what it is to have plenty. I have learned the secret to being content in any and every situation, whether well fed or hungry, whether living in plenty or want." Phil 4:12. I was learning very quickly that I had to just roll with the flow and I had to be full of joy and thanksgiving no matter what situation I find myself in because it's never about us, it's always about other people that are watching our lives and are seeing our attitudes and we are either going to encourage them or discourage them and I chose in this moment to use this situation to encourage others by maintaining my joy regardless. This would prove to be a theme for me over the next few months maintaining my joy because some things were going to come my way that were going to test that to the very core of my being. During all this God was still making ways out of no way I called my friend and told her what was going on and she was like it is crazy but right now I can't have you and the kids come here because there is alot going on and my heart just sank because here we are about to be homeless yet again, like why does this keep happening? Why is this the area of my life that I have had the biggest challenge and difficulty? I have some serious questions for the Lord and I'm trying not to be discouraged because all this is happening back to back without a real break and I'm doing my best to be strong and reassure the kids that God hasn't left us, he hasn't forgotten about us and that there is a reason for everything. My friend called back and was like if you can find an Airbnb I will pay for it and I was like ok that is a plan. I found an air BNB and we had it for a week so this gave me a little time to just whoosah my brain and figure out the next move whatever that may be. During this time we got a fateful call from Delaware and we found out that my nephew is in the hospital and he is in a Coma and it doesn't look good. I was like wait a minute Lord this wasn't part of the plan. Now this boy isn't my blood nephew but I have been a part of his life since he was 8 yrs old and him and my son were the best of friends like brothers I was with his Aunt for almost 8yrs and he was always at our house so at this point this boy is my nephew and I don't treat him like anything less than family I love this child like my very own children. I am devastated and my son isn't taking it well. These two were literally on the phone every single day since we were in Vegas and when we were back in Delaware they were always together they were inseparable. My heart is double brok at this point i'm hurt that my nephew is going through this but now my heart is broken seeing the pain in my son's face and watching him cry all I could do was pray that God heals his heart and that he does not allow this to make him bitter and angry at God. We are trying to find a way to get him back to Delaware and I didn't have a dime so it was going to have to be a miracle from the Lord. My son came with me to Tuesday night prayer, I could see how heavy this was weighing on his heart and he just wanted some relief. He just wanted God to heal him and all this to be over so they could talk about it and laugh. Now my son felt God telling him that he was going to use him to heal him and I believed that and I wanted my son to see the miracles of the Lord and allow God to use him. He begged the family to just leave him on the machine until my son got there. He was crying and called everyone that he knew that was there that could help them hang on just another day. I could feel the hopelessness in the voices of his parents, no one believes this family is so used to death and tragedy that they will not hold out hope for this vibrant 19 year old that could be healed completely. My son was so upset, I did everything I could to get him to Delaware as soon as possible. The church donated all the money that was needed for his plane ticket to Delaware. I even called the airline and moved his ticket up free of charge and that would get him to Philly by 1:00pm and they started surgery at 5am to remove his organs to donate and they ultimately let him die because they just didn't believe enough. I'm not judging anyones decision making but one thing I know for certain had that been my son, there would have been no way in the world that I would have took him off that machine after only 3 days I would have been in that room like in the movie John Q with my gun in my hand daring one person to touch that plug. I just couldn't imagine. I was crushed, my son took my anointing oil with him because he just knew that he was going to raise up after my son got there and prayed and anointed him. Seeing my baby boy's faith encouraged me and made me so proud of him. I couldn't help but be devastated. I could feel my son's heartbreak and it was making me so sad I was so angry at this family, all my son wanted was to see this boy one last time while his heart was still beating and they couldn't even give him that my heart broke for my son. Now this turned into a funeral trip and to watch the video of my son carrying that boys casket just broke me like an old porcelain plate. I cried my eyes out for days trying to understand why this was happening? What was going on why would you take this boy home so young. I was glad at the time that I was back at my friends house because I needed some prayer warriors around me, because my heart was broken and I was crying all the time because I just couldn't believe I would never see this child again, I would never see him graduate, never see his kids or watch him get married. This one really hurt and although I don't cry every day anymore I have learned that God's ways are not our ways and his thoughts not ours and we just have to trust our God is sovereign and that we will see this precious young man again. I can honestly say grief is the hardest thing to deal with because death is so final for us, although as believers we know that we will see him again, but trying to fathom that with our human mind that we will never see him again as we know it on earth is what makes the heart so heavy. I want to pause here and just talk to those that have lost someone that pain never really dies and time may help but it doesn't always get easier. My son still struggles and it was over a year in Aug and he is at his grave every day and still mourning, he told me that a piece of him died when my nephew passed and that is hard for me to take. I know my God is a comforter and a healer. I also know that he counts every tear we cry and he bottles it up. The bible says in Psalms he is close to the brokenhearted and he binds up their wounds and if you truly give your heart to him and let him come into whatever situation that you have he will heal you and take that heaviness from you. The bible says that He will give us a garment of praise for the spirit of heaviness. Not saying that we are going to praise God someone is gone but amidst the pain and anguish we can still call on the name of the Lord and maintain our peace and our joy regardless and that is what I had to do even in this situation which was a true test of my strength and fortitude. That is why I have to keep letting yall know nothing I was going through that I was dealing with my own strength because I wouldn't have been able to handle it. It's all God's spirit working on the inside of me helping me remember that I can do ALL things through Christ that Strengthens me. That is the one scripture I had to keep reminding myself of as I'm watching my faith be worked on in the operating room because these last few blows left me stunned and shaky and like any good fighter I have to take a few minutes to get my footing again so I can get back in the ring.

Chapter 19

Blow after Blow

My son comes back home from Delaware and he is just sick and depressed and I understand and i'm trying to give him a chance to grieve but I didn't want him to stay in this place for too long because he is my baby and I need him to be ok. This is not easy and he has never lost anyone in his life that he was this close too. Now a few of his friends were shot and one died in a car accident but the effects on him were not the same this hit different in so many ways because this was his brother for real they were kindred spirits. The moment I met that boy I knew him and my son would get along so good because they were so much alike and I was surely not wrong they were thick as thieves and they were truly joined at the hip even from 3000 miles away they facetimed each other 15 times a day. At this point we were back at my friends house sleeping on the couch and I was glad at this point we were there because it really gave us a support system that we wouldn't have had otherwise so it was a blessing. God is very strategic in what He does and how He does it. Although he doesn't cause these situations he definitely gets the glory out of each situation and he works it for our good. We are well into September and I'm still working at my job and I still have this car, the one I told you that was basically forgotten about by the rental car company it is nearly 5 months later and I haven't heard a thing, no one has tried to take any money out of my account and no one has even attempted to pick this car up so at this point I need it so i'm going to keep driving it. There is a slight issue though this car registration is about to expire on September 30 and I'm asking the Lord what I need to do next, show me what the next move is because I don't want to be outside of the will of

God. One Monday night after our women's group I decided to drop one of the ladies from the group off at home and this wasn't the first time I did this, we always talk for a while after and it's always a good time. It's getting really late and now its almost 11;30pm and im finally heading home now I will later find out that this car was reported stolen on September 16 but at this point I had no idea and i'm driving home like I did every night and all of a sudden I seen this car behind me and there was no lights one so at first I didn't think it was a State Trooper. I looked again and I noticed that it was now I am already a target because I'm here in Las Vegas and I have New York Plates so they were already with their antennas up. This guy must have followed me for 2 blocks and I was literally 3 mins from the house when this guy pulls me over, now he tried to make up some bogus reason for why he pulled me over that I was in the crosswalk or something like that who cares he pulled me over and now I have to figure out what is happening next. What was so funny is earlier that day I was at the park meditating and was participating in the Rosh Hashanah ritual of throwing bread into the water as a symbol of all the things you are going to let go and watch disappear. As I told yall before I was very in touch with my jewish and Hebrew roots and my time working at the Jewish school gave me the ability to study the different holidays and what they mean. So on this day along with my prayer time I did the ceremony and I just felt so light and ready for anything that was coming my way because I have truly laid all my burdens down. So Mr. Police officer was pulling me over and I asked him what was the problem, and he said this car was reported stolen and I needed to get out of the vehicle and he proceeded to arrest me and put me in handcuffs. I couldn't believe this but I went back to earlier that morning when I asked God to deal with this car situation since the inspection was expiring and I didn't know what else to do. He definitely fixed it, I explained to the officer what happened with the whole mix up at the rental car company and he listened and believed me and he thanked me for my cooperation and he was fairly decent to me. Until I told this man I had a loaded 9mm in my hand rest. He then found the gun and ran the serial numbers to make sure that it wasn't stolen and I just rolled my eyes and was like im not a thief the gun is mine and if you go in my wallet you will also see I have my license to carry a concealed weapon. He was nice enough to pack up my whole purse and all my things my two phones , my Ipad and all of my things that were in the front of that car and I appreciated that, even though I was in the back of this police car handcuffed God was still showing me favor he even let me call my son because he kept calling me because at this point it was after midnight and i'm never out this late so he knew something was wrong. I called my son and the first thing I said was that I'm a little bit arrested and I'm going to jail but hopefully I will be out right away just let everyone know and make sure you keep your sister calm. He knows his mom is a G and I have God on my side and I'm not scared. I'm actually laughing inside because what are the odds of me getting arrested and locked up on Rosh Hashanah. God was up to something and even though I didn't know what this would be a very significant part of this journey. Mr. Police officer thanked me for being cooperative and he did his best to treat me with respect and dignity and I was very thankful. I get to the jail and he has me take off my shoes and I have to put on these orange crocs that looked like they had not been washed in years and my OCD tendencies were really kicking in at this point and I was not feeling putting my foot in these shoes. I knew I had to so there was no room to protest Officer such and such was being as kind as that badge would allow so I had to bite this bullet and do what I was told so I can get this process over with. I'm so thankful it was a Monday night and not a Friday I would have been good and heated then, Im being processed and taken into the jail, this whole place looked filthy and I felt like if I touched anything I would instantly get Syphilis and I was praying for God to help me with these OCD tendencies because the closer I got to the inside of this place the more bugged out I became, I really needed the peace of God to wash over me so that I could deal with what was coming next. I get into this jail and I'm shackled hands and feet I don't know where they thought I was going but ok if this is how yall do it fine. I felt like I was going to be on an episode of the show jail because this place was a whole hot mess. It was jam packed and while I sat on this hard ass bench they are just rolling people in here by the van loads and I'm just like damn it's a Monday and this place is live as hell. I guess crime doesn't have a slow point and this is Las Vegas so I expected shenanigans. This was all new to me because I have never been in jail like this, I mean I was in a Reading Police Holding cell for 5 hours back in 1999 for a parking ticket but this was on another level. I really felt like I was in an episode of jail, the conditions in this place are awful the bathroom was so filthy and its CoED and there isn't a lock so anybody could just walk in there while doing your business so I had to wait until I couldn't hold it anymore and then I went and chile let me tell you I made it quick cause that place was about to have me itching and scratching it was so dirty.Im back in my jail jewelry waiting for someone to call my name for something I don't even know. It's now about 2am and I was sleepy but I won't be sleeping in this joint. There was a lot going on folks being strapped to chairs, people yelling coming down off highs like it was pure madness and of course the night wouldn't be complete if there wasn't a few prostitutes especially and old lady with a see through shirt on and no bra they had to give her a jail shirt because this was too much! If this place isn't good for anything it was definitely entertaining and I was wide awake and watching the show and just laughing, but even in the midst of this I had to ask God now that I am here what would you like me to do? There are a lot of hurt and broken people here and if you need me to minister just show me who and then they called my name, I went up and did my assessment and Got my blood drawn. Then it was mugshot time and yall already know I smiled a big old smile and served these coppers some face, dimples and teeth and had no shame in my game. After my mugshot they send me to the second processing area where you wait to be put in the holding cell with like 30 other women. As I sat there and started chatting it up with some of the ladies they brought some food and I took one look at that and said I'm fasting no thank you, went back to my seat. This lady was sitting across from me and she looked distraught so I started talking to her and in less then 10 minutes she had poured her whole heart out and I was now in full fledge ministry mode and I was encouraging this lady and before I knew it she started to cry and thank God that she talked to me, and I was like alright Lord I know now why im here so keep leading me. I could have sat there with an attitude mad at everyone because I was there on some BS but I kept my joy and allowed God to use me despite what was happening. I won't even lie, these conditions were deplorable and the COs in here are nasty. Once again I came in with a big smile on my face and no one can believe that I'm actually even in here because one of the COs asked me who I was and what I was doing there because I don't look like I belonged there. I wanted to say I definitely don't belong here. I didn't do a damn thing wrong. But I knew this was just another assignment and I was going to fulfill all God wanted me to even in a jail cell.I It was time for court and I was in a holding cell with a few of the ladies waiting on our turn for court and so I prayed with these ladies and one of the ladies started to cry because she was so afraid that she was going to lose her granddaughter. I prayed that God would send her a mighty blessing and show himself strong and give her favor with the judge. I watched the ladies go up that I was praying with and all of them had positive outcomes even the lady that thought she would lose her granddaughter and the judge said to her that she didn't even know why she was doing this but she was giving her another chance. I was just praising God on the inside for this lady and all the other women God was truly using me even in here and I was so thankful to be obedient. So it's finally my turn with the judge and court was at like 8am in the morning and I haven't even been to sleep yet, they are going to let me out without bail or anything but they were on such a backlog it would be the next morning before I am able to get out. Now after court they had me change into the prison blues, I had to strip and do all the humiliating shit that they make you do when you're locked up. I played this game though because I am here and I didn't have any other choice in the matter, I smiled though because although I was there I knew that, my God was on the throne and I will be out of here soon. This was all part of God's plan or if this was a weapon of the enemy it wasn't going to prosper. When I said yes to my Heavenly Father, that meant I was going to pick up my cross and follow Him. There was going to be opposition and persecution and I was going to be tested because at this point God wanted to make sure He could trust me, He wanted to make sure that I was prepared for all that was coming my way, every promise that God was about to fulfill in my life I needed this extensive preparation, for all the amazing things He had planned for me. I finally get upstairs into the population and out of the holding cell. I finally got to sleep, they woke us up at 1am to eat breakfast and I politely declined once I saw what was on the menu. I haven't eaten in 2 days and I barely slept. I definitely can't wait to get out of here. One thing I know is I don't know how people do months and years in this place, I was definitely not about this life. I love my freedom and all that entails but God needed to show me ministry translates all over so wherever I am I will do the work of the Lord in season and out of season because greater is He that is in me than He that is in the world. It was now about 6am on Day 2 and the CO woke me up to tell me that I was being released, can't say I wasn't ecstatic because I needed a good meal, a hot shower and about an 8 hr nap and I will be good as new. I was going to be happy to see the kids and let them know that I was alright. My son was definitely worried but he held me down and he called my spiritual mom and told her to pray because I was in jail. I was so proud of him though he held it together and made sure I was alright every time I called him. My friend was definitely a help and made sure my baby made it to school and was calm during this crazy time so in a way I was really glad and thankful that we were there at that time, God surely knows what He is doing even if we don't understand it. This was just another chapter in my life and another page in my book and although it was an awful ordeal God used all of this for my good and His glory in the middle of it all. I have to be back in court on Nov 5 so I was going to try and gather as much information as I possibly can so that I can get this crazy case dismissed because as of right now I didn't realize how much this arrest was going to affect me even if I'm not convicted. At this point I have now lost my job, I can't tell them that I was in jail the last two days and why I was a no call no show. This will prove to be a very tough season in the next upcoming months but God always has a plan and He is always by my side no matter what it looks like. These people that I was living with started to act funny, and even though no one was saying anything directly to me I could feel some definite tension in the camp and I wasn't for any of it. So now I was looking for the next instruction from my Heavenly Father and what my next assignment was because I didn't want to be anywhere I wasn't wanted or be out of God's grace. I know some of yall that will read this will say she really talks to God about everything and really thinks He is guiding her? Absolutely! There is not a time in my life since I truly gave God a Yes that I don't consult Him on everything because I never want to be outside of the will of God no matter what, I have lived the last 20 yrs outside of His will and suffered every single consequence and I will never do that again, there is too much at stake and I will not miss out on another blessing being disobedient or trying to do things my way.

Chapter 20

Tides are Turning

We have moved yet again, one of the families at our church welcomed us into their home after calling me and saying, I feel like God is telling us that you need to come here and stay with us for a while and I was like ok I will pray on it and see what happens and at the time I had a peace in my spirit. This was right on time, this will be my next assignment and I will do all that God is telling me to do. So when we get here we are all staying in the living room so we do not have any privacy, but i'm thankful that we aren't on the street but I am literally exhausted with the whole moving thing it's getting so old and tiresome. I have these candid conversations with the Lord and asked when Lord is all this going to come to an end? So that we can just be stable and comfortable again in our own space where no one will have the ability to just throw us out anytime they want because we are living with them. Now I am having some major conversations with the lady that we have moved in with and I felt as though God was really using me, and I see why I will be here briefly. I didn't have a car and have been trying to find another one and it just so happens that this family had an extra car that they have been trying to sell. One of the other amazing ladies at the church gave me 1300.00 she said God put it on her heart to do so and we ended up paying 1000.00 for the car and the other 300 would be for my insurance so this was truly a blessing and couldn't have come at a better time! God is so good and such a God of provision. To be back on the road was going to be such a blessing for us you have no idea so I did see God's hand at work in all of this. Being at the mercy of someone else is never ideal or fun so having our own car again was a huge weight off of our shoulders. I get the car and I take it to the shop to get an oil change and while there they give a free assessment of all the things that need to be fixed and this car needed more work done than I paid for the car so I would drive this until I couldn't anymore and then I would be getting a new one. It was old and it was a 2001 Ford Taurus and I didn't like Fords never even had one but I was thankful because right now it was getting us from point A to B and I wasn't going to complain.

The date comes up and it's time for court so I go in there not really knowing what to expect but I know that whatever happens God has it all under control but I was going to speak a miraculous dismissal over my life at this point. Now I do not have any representation because I technically don't have a case yet so I have no Public Defender. I'm on my own and when I go in and it was my turn the judge told me that the State had not picked up a case against me and that I was moving in the right direction. I didn't just want to settle for this and wait like a sitting duck for this racist state to decide to pick up a case against me, so I head to the law library the moment I leave court and I want to file a motion to dismiss. I just needed to know how. Being a part of this system in any way just disgusts me. I prided myself in keeping my record clean and staying out of trouble my whole life and this was a grave mishandling of the justice system and a waste of taxpayer money. I have all the necessary paperwork that I need to go back into court the next time on Feb 4 2020 and be able to let them have in the most educated way.

God knew I needed a little treat, a pick me up if you will, things were rough although I was handling it all with joy and grace I needed something to let me know God is still thinking about me and that He just wants to bless His daughter. I find out on Oct 23rd that my husband is going to be launching his Tshirt Line and that on November 17 he will be having a launch party at the store in California and he made it a point to let me know personally that he was going to be there between 2-4 and that I should pull up. I was like wait a minute Lord am I going to this? Send forth the finances that I need to go, if this is what I'm doing because seeing him right now would be everything in my life. I was super excited and giddy I could barely eat. I was so excited! These butterflies are back in full force. I couldn't control them. God is just so strategic and such a comedian, of all the times for this to happen it was now and I needed this so much. This whole weekend was special because my spiritual siblings were in town from Tampa for a Men's Conference at what would become my new church. Remember when I got that Prophecy months earlier about girding up my gift of the prophetic? This was the time, This will be the church and the Apostle over this church would become my spiritual mentor. I was at this conference and first my Brother and Sister in the spirit put 25$ in my hand, now you also remember I had prayed for these finances to come if I was going to LA on Sunday. This would be the first of the money that would show up. On Saturday I ended up getting an unexpected Venmo for 50$ from my Ex and then my son sent me 40$. I was like come on Jesus with these blessings I am going to see my husband!! This is now in motion, my nail tech that has been doing my nails for months had an opening and came that day to do my nails and my design matched my outfit that I was going to wear. It was all set and moving along nicely, I couldn't contain my excitement to see this beautiful man because it had been since March that I had seen him physically so this was going to be such a treat, and this is a more relaxed event so we will be able to talk a bit more and spend time together. I was ready, But these butterflies were in overdrive because I could not contain them. My friend also called me and said that she wanted to come with me and had 20$ for my gas so this was just getting better and better. The day is here and fortunately the people that I live with were not home so I was able to shower and do my hair because I wanted to straighten my hair because it had been a while. Chile if I knew it was going to be 91 degrees in LA that day I would have rethought that decision because by the time I got to this man I had sweated out my edges and I was trying to be cute with frizzy edges and that was not the look. I had to make it do what it do, I brought my hairspray and my brush so I brushed this hair, put on some more perfume and my lipgloss and was like its now or never I had texted our mutual friend earlier and let her know we are on our way, I had to stop at church first because I needed to get this good word before I see my husband and it was definitely a good word as it always is. Now we are heading to the mall and these damn butterflies are back in full effect and I feel like they brought about 600 more with them because they are just fluttering away in there.We get to the mall ad we start the journey to the store and ironically I had no trouble finding it and had only been there one other time. This was such a God moment and I loved every second of this. I am walking down this corridor at the Mall, and I see him in the distance and my knees get weak. I'm so nervous but excited and I'm so happy to see him again. I just wanted to give him the biggest hug. My son was with me, he wanted to check the scene. He told me straight up if this dude isn't feeling you or doesn't act like I think he should act then you need to leave him alone and forget about it. This child of mine was watching this man like a hawk already but he was doing his duty because my baby was not about to have his momma out here looking crazy, thirsty or none of the above so he needed to protect me. The closer we get to him my son says mom I can feel his nervous energy, he is actually really nervous to see you I can tell and now i'm just melting because im like how sweet is that! We finally got to the store, that was the longest walk of my life. I felt like I would never get there and my feet felt like I had lead in my shoes, these weak ass knees. We are at the store and when I walk up he immediately turns around and gives me a huge hug and I was taken by surprise because I didn't expect that at all. Then I see our mutual friend and she gives me a big hug as well and then tells everyone that I drove all the way out there from Vegas and then one of the ladies was like you drove all the way out here for this? I was like well first I came out here for church, but yes I would drive for them because they are my people and I support them. So then my husband asked me how you live in Vegas and have a church home in LA. I told him that my online church TPH One LA was my church when I came into town because I was a part of the online community and they are blessing my soul. He then said yea I know the Pastor he is great and I was like yes he is blessing my life with the series he is doing and it was on the Kingdom of God. So i Can tell that he was super excited at the fact I went to church and loved the Lord, it was almost like I could feel him making mental check marks in his head on all the things about me that he approves of . My son has been in the cut being Paparazzi and has taken at least 8 pictures of us and a video and I was laughing and I was so happy to see him. I just couldn't stop hugging him and clearly he was excited to see me too. I could tell this was going to be an amazing day, I couldn't believe I was standing here talking to him and just vibing. One of the ladies that was there asked me how old I was because I didn't look old enough to have a son that age, and I said he is my younger son. I have a son older than him and at the time my son was 24. She was like wow and I pointed to my shirt and said Black Don't Crack. He proceeded to say Facts it dont and I just started to giggle because that was his way of sending me a compliment. Indirectly and I will take it because I thought it was adorable, now this event is in full swing and im mingling with the other ladies there and talking with him and it's just a night that I never want to end. This same lady asked me what my nationality was because she just thought I was beautiful and she heard my accent. I told her what I was mixed with and I could feel him watching me out of the corner of my eye and I loved it and my son was like mom He really likes you, I could see him watching you talk while he was taking pictures with the other ladies but he couldn't stop watching you and I was like wow. I couldn't believe it but I wasn't surprised because I know how to work a room and I'm just being myself and allowing my personality to show and him to see me in all of my authenticity. I was makeup free because it was hot as hell out and I didn't want my face melting off and so he was getting all natural fresh face. I felt like he needed to see that because the other two times that I seen him I had a makeup on and I wanted him to see me without it and not that I need it, but I always wanted to put my very best foot forward when I see him and this time all though I was dressed up my hair was done with the exception of what had already sweated out because of this unseasonable heat in LA in November. My friend and my son and her grandson decided to go grab some food and leave me there with him. I feel like they saw us vibing and it was like she was in good hands. We can leave her for a while to talk to him. That is exactly what we did, we talked, we laughed, we took selfies and we had a great time. I enjoyed every part of him and this day we were really getting to know one another. So me being me I had to be a smart ass and call him out so I let him know" that card I gave you, I didn't put my number in there because last time I did that you never used it and I'm not giving you my number if you're not going to use it." He looked away and started turning red and was like well i'm busy and then I have my son and went in to all his reasons for not calling me. I said " How is one supposed to shoot their shot if you don't respond"? He didn't even know what to say after that and It was funny to me because I had him on the run, I had to let him know I don't care who you are. I'm not scared or intimidated and I'll tell you about yourself. Even though I was saying this my butterflies were telling on me because they haven't stopped since I got there and being this close to him isn't helping. Let me clarify something to all of my people reading this I have no problem holding people accountable even if I like them and they melt my heart, I wanted this man to know how you going to find a wife when people are shooting their shot and giving you numbers and you don't call clearly you cant want a wife that bad sir. Now we got into a whole other conversation and I asked him about coming to the Shelter and talking to my kids and the amazing impact that would have on them because his story is so powerful. He said oh yea my manager did tell me about that, so that was you? I was like yes it was and I just think the kids would really benefit from hearing your testimony and all that you have been through and look at you now they need these stories to give them hope. I said to him coming from where we come from we give them hope that they can do anything regardless and I told him that his story inspired me. So we spent the next 10 minutes talking about how he went to the detention centers and boys homes and ministered to those kids. This made my heart smile because I knew that our purposes were similar and we would be such a powerful force talking to these kids. God is just so amazing and He knows exactly how to choose our mates and when to put them into our lives I just couldn't believe it and I was literally standing in the confirmation of the Lord enjoying this blessing. We took some more pictures and I couldn't stop laughing and being silly. My friend was like wait let me suck my stomach in and then her face in that picture looked like she couldn't breathe and that made me laugh even more and at this point we had gotten extremely comfortable with one another and I was relentlessly flirting with this man and he was enjoying every minute I was laughing and laying my head on this shoulder just doing the most but listen I don't know when the next time is I will see this man so I was making the most out of this. He clearly was enjoying this as well because he was only supposed to be there for 2 hours and that turned into almost 4 hours and I didn't want this night to end it was clearly so needed and I just missed being with him and this was everything to me and will have me on Cloud 9 for the next few months. If at any other point in this journey I didn't believe this was my husband these moments today solidified all of that for me and I would never doubt my ability to hear the voice of the Lord clearly. One thing that I was becoming more comfortable with was hearing the voice of the Lord and watching Him perform in my life, the doubt that came in from what I heard concerning this man came from my own insecurities in the early part of this. I didn't see how this beautiful, well built man who can have any woman he wants would choose me, this was the lies the enemy loved to speak in my ear and I had to just shut him up. This man would choose me because God said so, not because this is what I want or think I should have because God said it and I trust Him with my life, every aspect and I'm not about to let the enemy talk me out of my blessing. I had to stay around people that could feed my faith and not my fear, the type of people that would believe this crazy thing right along with me and not try and sow seeds of doubt. This night ended with him hugging me one last time but looked like he wanted to say so much more, and he hesitated like he didn't want to go and everything inside me wanted to walk him out to his car and then get his number but I refrained from doing that and I just gave him a hug and he told me to drive safe and take care I could see how cute and protective he was being and it was so sexy. If I wasn't already super smitten with this man He has turned the heat up on me and I was just as giggy and school girlish as ever and I knew that at this point I was gone.

So the ride back to Vegas was a long one and just as God provided for us to get there he supernaturally provided for us to get back home too I was just in awe and I was so thankful for all that God was doing concerning this man and this relationship that we were establishing. I was literally smiling and giddy and I can not stop talking about him and this encounter because this was the best one yet and I was more than pleased with how this went. The fact that I had witnesses along with me that would not tell me what I wanted to hear but that would give me the truth because they love me and would never want me to make a fool of myself. They even said wow you guys are so adorable together, my son said that he really liked me and now he sees why God chose that man because we look really nice together and we were vibing. That made me feel so good because my son doesn't like anyone and he is a certified hater so this was really all I needed to hear because once I had his approval that was it I knew it was a done deal now I just needed God to give me the greenlight to move forward with communication at least. As well as this went, It would be a long time until I saw him again or had any real communication with him. Two days after our encounter my phone got turned off and I couldn't communicate, but this man had my email address if he really wanted to get in contact with me so now i'm back in the waiting room hoping that something will happen. I was trying to go back out to LA for a church even my other online church Change Church was having and it looked like it was going to be so good. I commented on one of his posts and let him know I was going to be back in LA on Dec the 8 and I would love to do lunch. Well this little innocent comment brought the trolls and stalkers out chile because someone hopped in my DMs and was basically trying to tell me this man was secretly seeing someone and they can tell im interested in him because im traveling to see him and all this nonsense, I very politely let this person have it and then made a PSA Post about these women being in my DMs and I tagged him in it. Little did I know then that he was very upset that someone would do that so he took it upon himself to also make a post basically chastising that person for trying to get information about us and to basically get a life preferably their own. I was like wow he is inadvertently defending me and it is super sweet and so romantic and that warmed my heart. That was the day that he restricted me on his page and I would know that then but would later find that out so I thought that he was ignoring me. I was so used to him liking my comments or commenting back and when I didn't see him doing that anymore I was like well damn what did I do. So me being me, I'm not begging nobody for shit and I'm not about to let somebody play me so I stopped going to his page. I was over it, I'm like if that's all it takes for him to ignore me then clearly I heard wrong and he isn't the one. I didn't know that he was actually protecting me and hiding me from the stalkers but I took offense and clearly I still had some maturing to do spiritually because I was being Petty Labelle. Months would go by with no interaction between us and now we are in a whole new year and a lot has happened in my life so let me backup a bit. The family that I was staying with had abruptly told me that we had to leave and we had until 4:30pm that afternoon to go and I was fine not to argue about it. God has a plan already in place so we would be gone. I had met this lady through my husband indirectly, she saw the picture I posted of us and she was like she knows him and she is just a regular person. So we spent hours talking on IG that night and I found out she lived here in Vegas and I was so surprised she said if you need anything at all even a place to stay please call me because I don't have much but I will share. So this whole conversation was the night before I will be told to leave, it's so amazing that this man was covering me and God was using him to open up doors for me because had this lady not followed him she would have never found me. The next day after I got that news I forwarded her the text and I said God must have known this and that is why He put that on your heart. I didn't know this lady from a can of paint but God was leading us to go there and I was going to follow the Holy Spirit and His guidance because this was clearly another assignment I was going on and it was an ontime blessing even if I didn't understand what was happening. At this point these people I was staying with were the last connection to this church and God had already told me to come out from among them and be separate so it was time to transition to the church God had led me to the weekend I saw my husband. It was official that Sunday I joined the church and I started attending every service regularly. Now don't get me wrong I didn't leave this other church with any bitterness or Ill feelings my time there was just up and everyone I was supposed to minister too and encounter I did I was very obedient and allowed God to use me mightily and that church had been a blessing for the time I was there but God seen the intentionality of the people and their hearts were not pure and there was a lot of stuff going on that I didn't have time to become a part of, so now it was time to move on because they received me not and so I had to knock the dust off my feet and keep it moving. I was on a mission from God and I didn't have time for people that couldn't see my worth or the anointing God had on my life. I wanted to be where I was celebrated and not tolerated so I am moving on with a clear conscience and a pure heart. What I need everyone to understand about these seasons of my life is that I am very intentional about doing God's Will, I do not want to sin against my Heavenly Father or do anything that would cause me to prolong what He wants to do for me or through me. Let me take this time out to say if we have not learned anything from the year 2020 God was truly deconstructing everything that man built for their own egos and not for God's glory. We have to be so rooted in God's word and His will for our life even if we do not always understand what is going on, God said in the word He will reveal His will to us we just have to be in the right place to hear it and obey. Back to the story it's now the end of 2019 for me and me and the children are basically living with a stranger but I was thankful that she opened up her home to me and my family and God was using this as a way to give us what we needed for the moment. I have moved more than 12 times in the year 2019 and to say I was exhausted was an understatement being constantly displaced was not a good feeling and being in spaces and places where people really didn't want you there was even worse so I had to just keep praying and seeking the face of God on what the next move was and how to make it happen.I could feel the prayers of my husband covering me and making ways for me as crazy as that may sound, this woman I wouldn't have even met if it wasn't for him so I knew that all of this was for a purpose I just had to figure out what that was. Things here were a bit frustrating for me and I prayed everyday because I knew that I was in a battle, the enemy was trying to steal my joy, my peace and my witness and I could not allow that. So we moved out of this ladies house and into what I thought was going to be a better situation for us and I needed 800 to move in and didn't realize that I needed that money prior to moving in and we have already moved out of this lady's house and had nowhere else to go and I refused to go backward and I called my Pastor and explained to her what was going on and I never heard back so that night we slept in the car and I remember crying as the kids were sleeping and asking God what this meant, how long will this be a part of my life having no place to lay your head was never fun, but when you have children that are looking for you to be the provider and the protector and all you can say to them is God got it, it is a scary situation especially to a child's mind that thinks you are crazy because you are trusting an invisible God that you may not even be sure exists with your life and your safety. At this moment all I can say is yes, I know He exists because I saw him work in my life, I have felt his presence when we were in car accidents, and when bullets came flying through my window. I knew my God was real and I was going to trust Him even if it didn't make sense to a natural mind. I knew that word was true that He would never leave us nor forsake us and I had to hold onto that with every fiber of my being. My spiritual mom called one of her long time friends that she remembered lived right here in Vegas and he was from our hometown and he knew my dad and my Uncles and I actually knew his daughter very well so this was definitely a blessing. He showed up and bought us food, Filled up my gas tank and put 100$ in my hand. I was so thankful! God is so good and He truly always provides. I was truly walking in my daily bread phase of this thing where God was literally giving me Manna from Heaven. Now I was able to get an AirBNB for the night at least so we can shower and sleep and revisit this in the morning. The next day was New Years Eve and I was going to be speaking at my church. This will be the first time I will ever bring a word from the Lord for the people and I wanted to be led by the Holy Spirit in every way. My sermon was called Identity Crisis and God really used me that night to bring a mighty word from the Lord to remind the people of who they are and what they have been called to do and all the power and authority we have In the Name Of Jesus. Service was amazing and it was so anointed and I could really feel the presence of God I didn't know though after where I was going to be going with my kids that night, but I knew that God was still on the throne and He was going to work it all out no matter what It looked like and that night we stopped at Del Taco to get some food and this particular one was open 24hrs and we ate our food and then we slept in the car that night and I told God this can not be how I bring this year in, I will not be without a place to go, this can not be the theme of this year too. I was really praying asking God what was the lesson that I needed to learn? What did I do that I was suffering the consequences of? When will this season of homelessness end? The answers I got in that moment were this is all for my Glory daughter and your good just endure, my strength will be made perfect in your weakness. After 2 days in the car my big brother and best friend called me and said I called a shelter and they have space for you please go there tonight after 6. I was trying to avoid the shelter but at this point I knew that this was the time and I wasn't going to fight or argue. This very shelter was the one that I used to volunteer at, and feed these people I was now being the one that was going to be fed and I was going to use this situation for the glory of the Lord. I could tell my daughter and son both were embarrassed and they didn't want to be there but at this point we didn't have any other choice. I know now as I am writing all of this it was God's way of humbling me and allowing me to break that habit I had of leaning on my own understanding. Trying to fix things or make things happen in my own strength those days were long gone and although I am obedient and I will go where god tells me to go and do what He tells me to do because faith without works is dead, I still needed to trust in my Heavenly Father because this was His will for my life not my own. I never in a million years would have moved to Las Vegas, I would have never willfully chosen to be in any of these situations, I wouldn't have even chosen this husband I had for myself. I would have stayed in

Delaware running my business and making things happen on my own, but God shut every door, stripped everything from me so all I had was Him to depend on and I knew that this was going to be another part of this book, I have endured all this fire, the refining fire of the Lord and at the end of all this I will not smell like smoke that is the promise God made to me. Look at how He took care of those 3 Hebrew boys that Got thrown in the furnace, because they would not bow down to the King and worship him. They said if we perish that ok because we will not sin against God and not only did the fire not kill them but Jesus was in that furnace with them and they came out without one single hair singed. This story always gives me hope because God's word is true and if we fully trust Him with our lives He will work everything out for our good and His glory it's all about our testimony. We are now at this shelter and it's not the most ideal situation but its provision and we are not worried about where we are going to sleep each night or how we are going to shower. My son was hating this whole experience because he was on the men's side because he is grown and those conditions were almost prison like and he was not for any of it and I felt for him but there was nothing I could do but pray. I knew that I had to make a decision when it came to sending my son back to Delaware although I love my baby and I really enjoyed having him here with me it was difficult because he was a grown man on paper and I couldn't keep carrying him because I was barely able to carry myself, and I felt like if your not helping me you are hindering me and I need a floatie at this stage of my life not an anchor. We are settling in, I am doing the Lord's work. I am ministering to people, showing the joy of the Lord in my life regardless of my circumstances and trying to bring hope where there is darkness. If I told you this was all sunshine and rainbows and everyone loved me I wouldn't be truthful I had a ton of hate and opposition coming from all over in that place. Darkness hates the light in God's people and although this place ran its business on the premise of God a lot of folks in that place staff included may have said Lord, Lord but their hearts were far from Him. During this time at this particular shelter God would use me in a mighty way despite all the opposition I faced. I cultivated some life long connections from being there and for that I was thankful. In February this car that I had that I told yall in previous chapters that I thought was a blessing will turn out to be less than that. As I was taking my daughter to school on the way to drop off my friend the car starts to struggle and then all this antifreeze starts to spill out of the car, thankfully when I pulled over I was at a tire place that also fixed cars so the guys came out and looked at my car and told me it looked like I had blown a head gasket. This is just wonderful, let's just keep adding things to this list so now I'm adding once again no car to the list. I'm like ok Lord what is the next move here? I had to quit my little job I just got because I was not going to be able to get my daughter to school and get to work on the bus. It's just impossible so that was that. God was once again strategically shifting things in my life. I was up every day at 4:30 am so that we could eat breakfast at 5am and we left at 6 so that I could get my daughter to school on time because this was a 2 hour bus ride. I love my baby and the only constant thing in her life was school and she had been there since the beginning of the year and I didn't want to disrupt that so If I had to inconvenience myself then it was ok. I would spend my time at the Starbucks around the corner from her school and just Write and plan and strategize and before I knew it time would pass and it would be time to pick her up and then we start this 2 hour journey back to the shelter. I met a lot of people during my time at Starbucks and I even got a gym membership so that I could work out and then shower before we went back to the Shelter. I was making the most of my time and occasionally God would send someone in my path that I could bless or that would bless me. Now it's March and we have been at this shelter almost 2 months and one of the staff comes to me and tells me that my son was getting put out, and I was like for what? Now at this point this particular chick had it out for me and my whole family she was truly being used as an instrument of the enemy but I wouldn't know how deep her hatred for me went until a little later. She proceeded to tell me that they found weed on my son and they were going to have to ask him to leave. Now did I think they were full of shit absolutely, did I think my son had weed? Possibly but is this something that warrants my 19 year old son being put out into the street over not at all. Then she had the audacity to ask me if I was going with him, I looked at her and laughed and said did you find weed on me? I have a daughter to think about. I'm not going anywhere, this will be the first time she will try to get me out. But one thing I know is that I serve a God that says He opens doors no man can shut so until God says it's over then and only then will I be leaving this place. I go tell my son what this lady told me and he goes straight to security and cusses them smooth out, so if I was going to be able to talk them into letting him stay he just sealed his fate so they let him get his stuff and 3 security dudes escorted my son off of the property. Thankfully he had made a few friends out here and went to stay with his homie while we figured this out. A few days later on March 5 I bought him a flight back to Delaware went to see him gave him a hug told him I loved him and that would be the end of my sons time here with me in Vegas, I was sad and relieved all at the same time I was going to miss him but I needed him to grow up and I couldn't keep allowing his attitude or his actions hinder what God was trying to do in my life. A few days later on March 9 we would get word that we were going into a full lockdown no one was allowed to leave for anything unless they were going to the hospital because this Covid 19 Virus was running rampant and the Governor put a shelter in place order in so He was shutting Vegas down. This meant school was going to be shut down and nothing was going to be the same as we know it. Everyone became all frantic and frustrated and I just went into prayer and allowed God to minister to me and give me my instructions. I started working 5 days a week in the kitchen. I would go in at 3am and work until 8am and on some days when we were short I would work until after lunch. I had met this cutie from The Bronx that was in the drug treatment program, now I know what you're thinking why would I be trying to date someone in a drug program. I wasn't trying to date him, I was just getting to know him because I liked his swag and he reminded me of home. We got each other and we could talk for hours and just laugh and have fun. I needed this and I liked the attention. I won't even lie, at this point I haven't had any communication at all with the husband and I didn't even know what was happening there and if God was raising someone else up. I just went with the flow of this because it was nice and we were definitely building a friendship and that was the foundation to any good relationship so I was going to see where this was going. He told me his story because he damn sure didn't look like a drug addict, so I wanted to know what the story was. He called me Queen and I loved that, he talked to me nice and he was so complimentary. He saw the greatness in me even in a place like that he knew I was different and I wasn't like the other woman and he appreciated that about me. We were working in the kitchen together and we would have a ton of laughs and that was exactly what I needed at this point of my life. This man was becoming a good friend and this was what I was missing. I needed all of this. Not long after the lockdown I was given a task of starting this childcare center for the shelter because now that the children were going to be doing virtual school they needed a quiet place to be able to do that. They had a building that basically was being used as a storage facility that needed to be cleaned out and organized and the CEO and the Director of Operations decided that this will be my task, I welcomed this new challenge with open arms this is where I flourish so if you don't want this to be successful then don't ask me to do it. So I was working in the kitchen in the morning and then on the building in the afternoon. I had gathered some people together to help me clean it out, move things out and put things together and because of who I was around there and the people respected me and the men just loved me I was able to recruit a lot of extra help.

Within 2 weeks I had this place ready for the kids to come in and make this a place to play and to learn and while doing this I started my P.A.C.K Program so I was making lemonade out of these lemons and I was ok with it. We have a meeting with all the parents and the staff and the Director gives me the floor and she basically said I was going to be the overseer and that I would then report directly to her. Someone didn't like that very much and wanted to interject her 2 cents in with the director as if I wasn't capable. The jealousy and opposition is so real. I proceeded to let the Parents and Staff know I had a degree in Early

Childhood education and I was also a Registered Behavior Technician and I have been working with children since 1999. Qualifications are not even an issue, just because I'm without a home and living in a shelter doesn't mean that I don't know what i'm doing or that I didn't have a professional life before I came there. This same lady that has been trying to get rid of me for months is still plotting on me and trying to destroy my credibility because she is intimidated by me because I could do her job and the one I was given better than her because when I work, I work for the Lord so everything I do I do with excellence. There was no holding me back or dimming my light and although many have tried they can not succeed, you can hate on me, you can lie on me but none of those weapons are even going to prosper and until I am done doing the work God sent me to do no one is going to get me out of there no matter how hard they try. And tried they did, I was harassed on a regular basis because I talked to alot of the guys, Now I have been celibate since Jan of 2019 and I have no desire to sleep with any of these men, not even my Bronx friend he was handsome and all that but he wasnt my husband so he wont be getting any of this cookie. In the late part of March there was a basketball game that the shelter did for the residents. It was a 3 on 3 and it was fun and it made things a lot lighter around there since we were all on lockdown and no one could leave. It was nice that they were letting us have fun. I was working security that day because they were short and I was filling in, now this was just another set up by the enemy to see how I was going to handle myself in these situations and I was frankly tired of people trying to play me like a sucka and I was letting folks have it in the most loving and professional way, but I was standing up for myself. After this game that my friend played in something had changed between us, he was avoiding me and I don't know what could have happened but I was going to get to the bottom of this. I texted him and he sent me back this weirdly cryptic text that wasn't even making sense to me. I just didn't get it but I had to keep remembering God is a jealous God and He will have nothing come before Him in anyway and I may have had my thoughts consumed by this man because it had been so long since someone that I was attracted to paid me attention and I may have gotten a little caught up so I had to repent and just keep doing what I was doing. I later would find out that the head of security threatened this dude that if he talked to me anymore he would get thrown out so this is why he abruptly stopped speaking to me and tried to make up some weird excuse for why he wasn't speaking to me anymore about one of the other guys in the shelter. This was all way too much who goes to this length to stop people from being friends. This got awkward and uncomfortable quickly. I was even sending notes with people I could trust to him and still no response and I felt a way so I was over it. Easter was coming so I was really busy in the Childcare center getting things ready for them. I wanted everyone in that place to get an easter basket of bags to feel special even if it was for one day. Easter Sunday I was on Quarantine because I had a sinus infection and was coughing a little so I couldn't be around anyone or the kids. I was telling the security how I wanted the easter egg hunt to go and how I wanted it organized and I didn't have on my mask and I started to cough and as I was backing up I tripped over the Cement Parking stopper (if that's even what its called) The guys pick me up and I keep talking even though my right wrist and arm is hurting so bad I go back upstairs to my room and I facetimed my sister and was like sis look at my arm is this broke. She was like um yeah it is now go to the hospital and get it imaged because that doesn't look good. So I go shower and get dressed and then I go to one of my favorite staff members that actually has had my back since the beginning and I just loved her to pieces, she was definitely a bright spot in that place and i'm so glad God sent her my way she was definitely my angel. I say to her well I think my wrist is a little bit broken and she was like what? You need to go to the hospital like now. So she went to the boss and we showed him my arm and he allowed her to take me to the hospital. I got my xray and found out not only did I break this wrist, I fractured it in 4 different places and if it didn't heal properly I was going to need surgery. I immediately started praying and speaking healing over myself because I was not getting another surgery. I am now in alot of pain, I have an appointment to see a specialist so that I can get casted and have them closely watch me healing process, this was the first time in my 42 years that I had ever broken a bone I was like of all the times for this to happen it had to be now. But God had a plan and a purpose for this because he sees the end from the beginning. I get my cast and of course it's purple and all my people start signing their names on it and it becomes a whole thing. This will definitely be an Easter Sunday for the books. I couldn't even eat because this was my dominant hand. I immediately started practicing my writing with my left hand so that I could sign all my own papers and not need so much help. I learned how to dress myself, and do my own hair because I didn't want to be dependent on any one. Ten days after I broke my wrist i'm still dealing with shenanigans and peoples nonsense folks are messing with my daughter and lying on her and it's just too much they think because I have this arm dilemma that I still won't beat someone down, they better ask about me when it comes to my baby its going to be a whole problem. I let them know I was not going back into that child care center. I don't want to be around anyone or their children. I'm in alot of pain and I just need to rest. So the days that I wasn't even in the center the head of security and this staff member that doesn't like me conjured up this story that me and my daughter were hitting peoples kids and putting them in the bathroom for time out. The worst part of this all is that the one person in there that I thought was my friend that I could talk to and that I was always there for betrayed me and went along with this lie knowing it wasn't true. I get called into the office with my daughter and they asked us what happen and we told the truth I wrote a statement and everything and a few hours later the police show up and i'm sitting their joking like it wasnt me this time, then all of a sudden security comes over and tells me that we are being transferred to another shelter I was like what, why? The cops then ask me about myself and my daughter hitting someone's child and I just start to laugh and say sir I have a broken wrist, I dont hit my own child I would never hit anyone elses child and my daughter is 14 what does she look like hitting on a baby. I proceeded to tell this officer this is what happens when you decline all the advances of the head of security and when you can do people's job better than them they get intimidated and have to make up lies to get rid of you. I went up stairs and backed up my stuff as fast as I could with the use of one arm and packed up that police car, at this point these officers are laughing and joking with me and they said no one is pressing charges on you or your daughter so I guess i'm just your ride to your next destination. We said our goodbyes to everyone and people were crying. My daughter was crying and even some of the staff was sad to see us go. It was the beginning of a beautiful transition where God was going to show himself strong in my life and allow His will to be done fully in my life. This experience would definitely prove to be very traumatic for my daughter who has had quite a year already and it's only April but this next venture would be our road to healing. So on April 22nd we moved on to a women's shelter and this would prove to be a blessing in disguise. I can't lie, this sting of betrayal and persecution took a toll on me and my heart felt a bit broken. Then to hear that my friend was literally crying when he heard that they were putting me out that made me sad too. I had a lot of feelings to process through and I needed God to step iI wrote my friend 2 letters when I got to the other shelter because I felt now that i'm not their He will want to talk to me now but I never got a response to either letter and that was it for me I was making the transition to forgetting this man and focusing on my healing and allowing God to speak into my spirit and show me what I needed to do next. One thing that I did when I got to this shelter was stay to myself I didn't talk to anyone but staff, I had made a friend when I was in the isolation trailer and then she was gone so that was it for that, I felt that God was showing me to just stay to myself and allow Him to heal my heart and speak to me because at this point I got a little bruised in this last fight so I needed God to tend to my wounds. I kept these headphones in and kept this music blasting into my ears and just allowed that to take me to another place. During this time I started spending a lot of time on Instagram because I noticed since the lockdown alot of celebrities that you may not see online were online and interacting more with the people so I was going to see what this was about. In May I started to really make my mark on IG. I started going on live tours like my son likes to say and I got to talk to some pretty amazing and major celebrities. I was making my presence known and I also was showing people my bubbly and amazing personality. I also started sharing my story about being in the shelter and not because I wanted someone to feel sorry for me I wanted them to see that my joy went beyond my circumstances and I wanted to bring encouragement to other people. A few weeks later God had put on my heart that I was going to start doing my own live shows and I was going to just encourage and bring a word from the Lord. I started going live just on a Tuesday and I was playing around with different times so that I can reach the best audience at the right time. I didn't even know how to start a live, I had to call my son and have him walk me through it and he was so sick of me because I called him 3 times because I couldn't find the live button, finally I found it and I went for about 7 mins. The next week I would go live for a little longer, and then eventually I started doing the full hour and even learned how to bring people in and it became so much fun. During this time my friend sends me a message and tells me that my husband was going live every week since March and that he brings people in and it was fun, she said but I feel like he is looking for someone, like that he is looking for you. I was like really? He hasn't forgotten about me? I was instantly smiling and excited and it gave me the insight of why any of those guys I was talking too didn't last. I go on that live for the first time and the first thing he does is shout me out first and last name chile, the whole entire government I was like oh ok this is what we are doing? That night he brought my friend on and she was so happy she was like you were my good luck charm I have been trying for months to get on there and then the first time you came on he brought me on she was like it was all because of you. She is one of the few people that know about me and him and she doesnt think I'm a nutcase. She is so supportive and actually is always there with reassurance and I appreciate her so much. I am now invested and I am tuning in every week and watching to see if he will pull me in and most of the time I'm looking presentable so it's all good. Well on Pentecost Sunday May 31 I was tuning in and as always I click the button just in case. Now I said a prayer 2 days ago and I asked God to make a way for us to communicate if this man is really the man that He has chosen for me. That day I was just minding my business, I had a ratchet bun and workout clothes on and was not anticipating being brought on. All of a sudden I seen the circle going around which meant he accepted my request to go live and I literally was gasping for air when I popped up on the screen and he looked nervous and I started cheesing and we talked briefly I made a toast and picked a song, My song was Luther Vandross Take you out, one of my favorites but also a hidden message in that song just for him. I was on Cloud 9 once again. That was the best 2 minutes of this year and I was so thankful that God was still giving me the signs and showing me that this was the man I just needed to stay focused and allow God to do His work because His timing is perfect. So every week after that he would make it a point to talk to me in the chat, answer one of my questions or play a song that spoke to my heart. This has become my favorite part of the week and I was so thankful for him and his vulnerability and transparency in these lives. He was really giving me a front row seat into his life and it was beautiful and so God ordained. The spiritual connection that we still share has never really been broken. I was still praying for him even if I wasn't speaking to him because I heard what God said and that is what I wanted to believe above everything else. Now I am doing my lives and I am meeting so many amazing people in these IG streets and in June I met a DJ that became what I thought was a friend but I will learn real quick everything online isn't what it appears to be and no matter how much you think you know someone and can trust them you can't and so we started doing a Show on IG live together called Think Light Talk Heavy and we talked about alot of different topics and had a lot of light and funny back and forth banter. I lied to him and our on screen chemistry was definitely something the people liked to see. As we got closer and deeper into the show we would talk alot and the first show we did was like a 7 hr marathon and we just had a ball and I couldn't wait until the next one. Now at this time i'm still making all these different celebrity connections and just living my best life out here in these IG streets. One night me and this dude have a falling out because I basically told him it would be nice if he could call me back so we could discuss show ideas and chile this brotha goes off the deep end on me and tells me that he doesn't belong to me and that I need to stop expecting him to just drop everything and call him back and that until further notice the show would be on pause. I told that brotha straight up I don't need you and you can put yourself on pause but the show would still go on with or without you and that was the best thing that man could have done because that opened up the door for me to have some amazing guests on my show and have some amazing conversations. So in Aug I started a Classic Hip Hop series on the show where I brought some of the most Iconic pioneers of our time and it was a pleasure to talk to them and learn about the side of the game no one talks about. I realized I had a gift for this and this was a lane I was creating on my own without anyone's help, I was finding and booking these artists and setting up the shows and framing the conversations and week after week I am blessing and educating the people and paying homage to the Hip Hop culture. I then Started a second IG live show called Girl Chat Friday and I had some of the most amazing female guests and some celebrities and some regular people but all just amazing conversations and enlightenment and encouragement for all of my people viewing. I didn't understand what this meant and what was going to happen when God said just start going live and let me do the rest. No one in their right mind would have started doing IG live shows while living in a homeless shelter, but this became my passion and my job I had a duty to the people and I wouldn't let them down I would show up every night I was scheduled on time, hair done, dressed cute lip gloss popping and gum cracking this was who I was and I found an outlet to be myself and the people loved it and although the gifts and the Cashapps I recieve are a blessing what I love more than anything are the messages I get that tell me how I have changed their life, How something I said changed the way they looked at their circumstances that is why I started doing this and I wouldn't trade it for anything. Although 2020 was quite a year it cultivated some of the most beautiful relationships that I have made life long and it's all God's favor over my life and me walking in my purpose. Gods provision over my life in the midst of a pandemic has been tremendous and even at the shelter no one is even allowed to do anytime of video chats or social media videos for the sake of the privacy of the residents but i always found an isolated spot and did each one of my shows and no one ever bothered me and it was a blessing God had his favor over my life and even some of the ladies that lived their started to watch my shows and were blessed by it and that is why I kept pushing on even when I didn't feel like it or even when I was dealing with my own disappointments and setbacks I still made a consistent effort to come on as scheduled and be a blessing to the people. During this journey I have made it a point that whatever state I was in to be productive in some way or another during this time of waiting I became the best me I could become As of today I am down 75lbs, I have walked fully into my purpose and I watched God turn a situation meant to break me down, make me bitter and depressed and he gave me joy unspeakable and for that I am thankful. I wish I had some magic antidote to this life that will just instantly make everything better but all I can tell you as I bring this book to a close is that in the middle of it all be your greatest self do not let anyone tell you who you are not or what you can't do. Step out on faith and watch God turn every situation designed for evil and make it good and make it work for you. On Dec 6 My daughter and I both were diagnosed with COVID and if this would have been the ending to my 2020 fortunately we were not nearly as sick as everyone else had gotten and I know that is all Gods grace and mercy and his healing power at work but on Dec 7 after almost 12 months in the shelter system they move us out and into isolation housing which ended up for us being our temporary housing so we don't have to go back to the shelter. I kept saying I wanted to be out of there by Christmas I wanted to give my daughter the gift of being in our own space and God did exactly that we were in our own space for Christmas and New Years and I was able to cook my own dinner for the first time in a year and it was such a joyous and monumental occasion. So whatever you do as you read this, do not ever give up, no matter how hard it gets do not let anything stop you from reaching your goals. Watch your tongue and speak life over yourself and every situation you find yourself in. It's never too late as long as you have breath in your body to reach all of your goals and get all that God has for you. This New Year 2021 I will receive all that He has for me according to His will not mine so I will continue to patiently wait for this beautiful man to fully show up in my life so we can fulfill God's purpose for our lives and we can do all He has called us to do so stay tuned and stay plugged into all the amazing things God wants to bring into your life in this year and the years to come Keep the faith and do not let anything shake you In the middle of it all.

Acknowledgements:

I want to thank my big brother Kenny Burns for this amazing note he wrote me:

"I look forward to that smile and energy and that gum poppin daily Keep Going- Kenny Burns Lifestyle Specialist

My son Daivion Brown:

"My mom has made some mistakes, what parent does not? But it's not about how big the mistake is, it's how she acknowledges how it affects her children and tries everything in her power to not put us through that again. When she had nothing she made sure we had everything. She is the strongest woman I know and will remain Number 1." -Daivion Brown

My Spiritual Mother:

"Jamie has come such a long way and I have known Jamie more than Half her life, she is the person that takes a change that is also a challenge and she chooses by faith to embrace the challenge which causes her to triumph." -Betty Williams Author of Getting Unstuck on Amazon

CPSIA information can be obtained
at www.ICGtesting.com
Printed in the USA
BVHW091615300321
603711BV00007B/1265